D0859730

Institute of Criminology, University of Cambridge

CAMBRIDGE STUDIES IN CRIMINOLOGY

EDITED BY

L. RADZINOWICZ, LL.D.

VOLUME XIX

THE HABITUAL PRISONER

THE HABITUAL PRISONER

An Enquiry by the Cambridge Institute of Criminology

CARRIED OUT BY

D. J. WEST, M.D., D.P.M.

ASSISTANT DIRECTOR OF RESEARCH IN THE INSTITUTE

LONDON

MACMILLAN & CO LTD

NEW YORK · ST MARTIN'S PRESS

1963

MACMILLAN AND COMPANY LIMITED
St Martin's Street London WC 2
also Bombay Calcutta Madras Melbourne

THE MACMILLAN COMPANY OF CANADA LIMITED
Toronto

ST MARTIN'S PRESS INC
New York

PRINTED IN GREAT BRITAIN

CONTENTS

PREFACE

BY THE DIRECTOR OF THE INSTITUTE

THIS report presents the results of the first enquiries carried out by Dr. D. J. West since he joined the Institute of Criminology. His interest has centred upon psychological and psychiatric aspects of criminal behaviour.

His report is concerned with the habitual prisoner, a subject which would be topical at any time. The Prevention of Crime Act of 1908, the Departmental Committee on Persistent Offenders of 1932, the Criminal Justice Act of 1948, represent successive stages in the attempt to come to terms with the obdurate problem of the recidivist. Now, after more than half a century, the Advisory Council on the Treatment of Offenders has been asked to review the whole question again. At this juncture, when we seem once more to be at a dead end, Dr. West's study cannot fail to evoke great interest.

It brings forward fresh and important evidence that the basis of our legislative and administrative approach to the problem of the persistent offender is inadequate and distorted. A no less valuable feature of the enquiry is the way in which the social and clinical interpretations have been blended, so that the findings have the impact of real human situations.

We wish to express our appreciation to Mrs. Audrey Smith, psychiatric social worker, who visited relatives, collected the documentary records and collaborated in the analysis of the material; to Dr. J. Field, for the results of tests used in a section of this enquiry; to Dr. W. H. Hammond, of the Home Office Research Unit, for some of the data about men undergoing preventive detention; to Mr. R. S. Taylor, Senior Psychologist, H.M. Prison, Wandsworth, for additional psychological testing and helpful advice; to Chief Superintendent Crayfourd and the staff of the Criminal Record Office, Scotland Yard; to H.M. Prison Commissioners and to the staffs at H.M. Prisons, Wandsworth, Parkhurst,

Nottingham, Chelmsford and Eastchurch, for making it possible to carry out the enquiry; to the Central After-Care Association, to the record offices of the three armed services, and to various hospitals, probation officers and social agencies, for their ungrudging help.

L.R.

INSTITUTE OF CRIMINOLOGY
UNIVERSITY OF CAMBRIDGE
October 1962

INTRODUCTION

THE raw material for this study consisted of two series of prisoners, a group of fifty men serving sentences of preventive detention, and another group of fifty men, all of them recidivists, serving sentence of imprisonment at Wandsworth. Preventive detainees were chosen because they represent the 'end of the line' so far as penal treatments are concerned. They are men who have had so many convictions and punishments that it is felt nothing is left to do except to shut them away in safe custody for a very long time in order to prevent further harm to the community. It was anticipated that these hard cases would provide useful material for the study of psychopathic personality. The second group, the recidivists at Wandsworth, were specially selected on account of an apparent intermission in their criminal careers. They had all had at least one substantial period of years free from criminal convictions, although at other times, both before and after, they were repeatedly caught and sentenced. It was hoped to explore the circumstances associated with crime-free periods in otherwise persistent offenders.

While carrying out these two enquiries, it became apparent that the two groups, the preventive detainees and the intermittent recidivists, bore striking resemblances. The nature and scope of the crimes, the almost exclusive concentration upon offences against property, the motivations involved, and the personal peculiarities of the criminals, were much the same in both. It seemed probable that most offenders with a long history of frequent convictions and imprisonments might show these same features, and so it was decided to present the findings in the form of a survey of the psychiatric characteristics of the habitual prisoner.

This term, which appears in the title, was preferred to the more usual 'habitual offender', since one of the most prominent characteristics of both series of prisoners was being repeatedly apprehended and imprisoned. In a few cases the habit amounted to deliberately seeking arrest. Among such unfortunates the petty thief predominated over the skilled operator. The determined professional criminal, however persistent his anti-social activities, rarely sinks to the status of a habitual prisoner.

The series of preventive detainees were studied in greater detail and at greater length than the fifty Wandsworth recidivists, in which group the crime-free periods provided the focus of interest. Furthermore, since the Wandsworth group had been selected on account of their intermittent records, they may not have represented altogether typical recidivists. In the report that follows, therefore, the findings concerning preventive detainees constitute the main result, in both text and tabulations, with the corresponding findings on Wandsworth recidivists utilised, when available, for supportive evidence and for purposes of comparison.

For ease of reference, the Wandsworth recidivists, who were seen first, have been numbered 1 to 50, and the preventive detainees 51 to 100. References to individual cases are indicated by the numbers in parentheses, and some particulars of each case are given in the key Table 18. A list of the cases mentioned in the text appears in Appendix II.

D.J.W.

INSTITUTE OF CRIMINOLOGY
UNIVERSITY OF CAMBRIDGE
October 1962

I

COMPOSITION OF THE GROUP

1. Preventive Detainees

PERMISSION was obtained to interview men serving sentences of preventive detention. According to the Criminal Justice Act, 1948, *S.* 21, offenders convicted on indictment for an offence punishable by two or more years' imprisonment are liable to sentences of five to fourteen years' detention if they have reached thirty years of age and have been similarly convicted on at least three previous occasions since the age of seventeen and have already been sentenced at least twice to terms of imprisonment, Borstal training or corrective training. This section provides means for confining the persistent offender for longer than would ordinarily occur as punishment for his latest offence. The Act specifies that the provision should be used when 'the court is satisfied it is expedient for the protection of the public'.

By definition, therefore, preventive detainees are recidivists of mature age. In practice, although large numbers qualify for consideration, the courts tend to choose this method of disposal for the most persistent of offenders against property, those with the greatest number and frequency of convictions. A relatively trivial offence may lead to a long period of detention if the offender has a long record, but in recent years there have been some successful appeals on the grounds that the sentence of preventive detention was disproportionate to the gravity of the offence.

The prisoners utilised for the survey consisted of a series of fifty-one men all of whom had undergone conditioning tests and personality tests administered by a research psychologist, Dr J. G. Field, who was at the time on the staff of the Institute of Psychiatry, London. This group was chosen so that the psychiatric findings could be compared with the results of previous testing. All the psychiatric assessments were completed and tabulated before Dr Field communicated the results of his tests, so that any correlations would not be due to unintentional bias. The tests took place at the allocation centre at Wandsworth Prison, through which all detainees pass before placement in one of the four central prisons which house them during the second stage of their sentence. Since the men were in any event partaking in psychological tests as part of the allocation centre routine, the introduction of additional tests presented no particular difficulty. The preventive detainees arrive at the allocation centre approximately a year after conviction. The sample included a few sentenced at the very end of 1956, but the majority had been sentenced during the first half of 1957.

The prisoners tested by Dr Field were substantially unselected, consisting, in principle, of blocks of consecutive admissions to the Wandsworth allocation centre during the periods of time covered by his investigation.

Dr Field writes as follows on this point:

> 'The ideal selection method would have been the investigation of every case as cases arrived in the appropriate part of the prison. This method would avoid the problem of selection altogether. Because of the many demands made on the time of inmates (by medical examinations, visitors, interviews, disciplinary deprivations, etc.) this was impracticable. Instead the following approximation was adopted.
>
> 'The men arrived at the appropriate part of the prison in batches, generally numbering from four to eight. Testing would commence with the case bearing the lowest number in the batch, and the rest of the batch would be tested in the ascending order of their P.D. numbers. If a man was not available for testing the rest of the batch was not tested until the man did become available. If the man did not become available during the period that the batch remained in the appropriate part of the prison the remainder of the batch was not tested.'[1]

It would appear that the factors responsible for the selection were unrelated to penal history and personal characteristics, and there is no reason to suppose the sample unrepresentative.

2. Intermittent Recidivists

Permission was sought and obtained to interview men serving sentences in Wandsworth Prison. This institution does not normally admit first offenders, and therefore has a relatively high proportion of recidivists. Men sentenced to longer than four years'

[1] In practice, those selected consisted of men with serial numbers commencing 0 and finishing 150, in the following batches: 0 to 6 complete, 22 to 29 complete, 40 to 54 complete except for two, 120 to 130 complete, 142 to 150 complete, plus 13 others in smaller batches. From this total ten were excluded because, although they received some psychological tests, they were not available for or not given the conditioning tests.

imprisonment are usually sent to other prisons. The prisoners were selected solely on the basis of their criminal records. The files at Wandsworth Prison were searched for men with 'gaps' in their records of convictions. For this purpose a 'gap' was defined as a period of at least four years at liberty and free from convictions, preceded by criminal convictions on at least two occasions in adult courts, and succeeded by at least two further subsequent convictions. The reasons for these criteria call for some explanation.

Conviction-free periods due to imprisonment were of no interest. Periods under detention in penal establishments were therefore discounted, and had to be subtracted from the intervals between convictions in order to determine the periods at liberty. The intention was to discover and study instances of intermissions in the criminal careers of established adult offenders. For this reason convictions as juveniles under the age of seventeen were disregarded and the proviso was made that the conviction-free period should be preceded by at least two convictions as an adult before it could be regarded as a gap in the course of an established criminal career. It has been suggested that a typical criminal career has a natural span of seven years, after which offences tend to diminish or cease altogether. The reason for stipulating at least two convictions subsequent to the conviction-free period was to exclude instances of an isolated lapse in men whose criminal careers were virtually at an end.

The decision to consider only substantial periods exceeding four years was taken because such long intervals are exceptional and may therefore be thought more probably connected with special circumstances. The limit of four years was based on experience communicated by Dr Hammond of the Home Office Research Unit. In the course of a survey of records of offenders liable to preventive detention, who had an average of fifteen convictions per man, Dr Hammond found that ninety per cent had been re-convicted after less than four years at liberty, and seventy-three per cent had been re-convicted after less than two years.

Approximately eight per cent of the criminal records of prisoners serving sentences at Wandsworth were found to have one or more 'gaps' fulfilling the criteria described. These criteria comprised the minimum requirements for inclusion of the prisoner in the study. Of course many of those examined had gaps of much longer than four years, preceded and followed by considerably more than two convictions.

The files were examined in alphabetical order, and all those found to have 'gaps' were extracted, up to a total of fifty cases. Only two files had to be rejected and replaced by others, one because the prisoner was in hospital and not fit to be interviewed, the other because the man was transferred to another prison before his turn came to be seen. The fifty men interviewed therefore comprised an unselected sample from the population of prisoners at Wandsworth who had 'gaps' in their criminal records.

II

METHOD OF ENQUIRY

1. Psychiatric Interviews

An attempt was made to see every prisoner at least once, and also to visit their homes and interview a relative. The psychiatric interviews with the men I undertook in every case myself, but the home visits, in all but five cases, were carried out by Audrey Smith, a psychiatric social worker with long experience of prison work. For geographical reasons, visits to the homes of two of the preventive detainees were carried out by social workers residing in Scotland and Eire, and I visited the homes of three of the intermittent recidivists when Audrey Smith was otherwise engaged.

Interviews took place with all fifty of the intermittent recidivists and with forty-seven of the fifty-one preventive detainees. Although a few showed reluctance at first, and two swore aggressively that they would never answer personal questions, all those interviewed did in fact provide some account of their life history. The four missing preventive detainees consisted of one man (69) who declined to co-operate in an extended interview and walked out of the room, two who had died in the three-year interval between Dr Field's tests and the present enquiry, and one who had escaped from detention following transfer to a mental hospital (33). A prison medical officer who had known one of the deceased men intimately volunteered a detailed description. Information about the escapee was provided by the mental hospital concerned. This left only one deceased man for whom no informant could be traced and there was no information to supplement the penal records. It was therefore decided to omit that case, and to base the investigation and the tabulations on the round number of fifty preventive detainees.

The intermittent recidivists were interviewed at Wandsworth Prison and the preventive detainees at the Central Prisons at Parkhurst, Nottingham, Eastchurch and Chelmsford. Two psychotic detainees were seen elsewhere, one at the psychiatric unit at Wormwood Scrubs Prison, and the other at an outside mental hospital. The interviews with the recidivists at Wandsworth took place at all stages of their imprisonment, those with the preventive detainees took place three to four years from the commencement of their detention. At each of the institutions concerned, a private room was provided and talks with the prisoners could continue as long as required. At Wandsworth the prisoners were seen for two to three hours, the longer periods being spread over two interviews. Sometimes the second interviews were simply a continuation of the first, sometimes they were used to clear up discrepancies between the prisoner's previous statements and information obtained subsequently from other sources. The preventive detainees were seen for rather longer periods, from two and a half to four and a half hours, spread over two or more occasions when necessary.

The prisoners were summoned to the interview room by a prison officer, and so far as is known they were simply told that a doctor wished to see them, leaving him to explain in his own way the purpose of the interview. At Wandsworth the summons generally came to the men unexpectedly, but at the preventive detention centres, once interviewing commenced, news quickly spread, and one was occasionally greeted with remarks like 'I know you come from the criminology people!'

Each initial interview commenced with a short set speech by way of explanation. This was given in more or less the same words each time, but varying or repeating the sentences if the prisoner broke in or appeared not to follow.[1]

Some prisoners were suspicious and asked questions such as: 'How did you pick me out?' 'What does it all lead to?' 'Will it help me at all?' The prisoners' questions were always answered as fully as possible, but without laying stress on any particular aspect of their lives or problems.

The interviews with the prisoners and their relatives did not follow an unvarying sequence or include a formal series of questions. Instead, by utilising the time-honoured psychiatric tech-

[1] The explanation ran as follows: 'Please sit down. I am Dr West, and I am a psychiatrist. I have been coming to the prisons to do some research work. All we are really trying to do is to find out some of the reasons why some people get into a lot of trouble and others manage to keep out of it. And so I've been seeing people in here and asking them to help by telling me about themselves. So far everybody I've seen has done so, and I'm hoping you will too. But I must explain that anything you tell me is confidential, between ourselves. I come from outside — I work for a University — and I've nothing to do with the prison service. And I am a doctor, so that even if I wanted to give any information I wouldn't be allowed to.'

nique of posing topics in preference to direct questions, the interviewers set out to obtain accounts, as spontaneous as possible, of various aspects of the prisoners' lives. With the prisoners themselves the topics of chief concern included recollections of early upbringing and relationships with parents, experiences during school, work and service careers, the onset of dishonest or anti-social habits, sexual and marital adjustment, outstanding features of character and temperament, symptoms of psychosis or neurosis, the prisoner's chief interests and general style of life when out of custody, and his attitudes to his offences. The questions concerning criminal behaviour were put as opportunity arose. For example, questions about truancy and juvenile delinquency were raised at the same time as questions about performance at school and in sports. The process and sequence of history-taking was adapted to individual attitudes and intelligence levels, but always with the same general scheme in mind. The intention was to build up the mens' confidence by showing a genuine interest in their whole life and background into which the offences might be fitted as part of the total picture. Towards the end of some of the interviews with the intermittent recidivists, in cases in which the required information had not emerged spontaneously, direct questions were put to the prisoners about conviction-free periods, including whether the prisoner himself thought that they coincided with anything or had any particular significance.

2. Home Visits

Towards the end of the first interview, the prisoners were asked if there was someone outside who knew them well who could be seen by a social worker. This request was sometimes met with considerable suspicion, especially perhaps by those prisoners who had given untruthful histories. It was generally explained that other people see us differently from the way we see ourselves, and that for a psychiatrist to understand problems he must have the other person's viewpoint as well. The prisoners could not all be persuaded to agree to this, but without their consent the Prison Commissioners do not permit prisoners' relatives to be communicated with or asked to grant an interview. It may be that some of the men would have given somewhat different stories had they known from the start that outside enquiries were to be made. A few of the prisoners, although consenting formally to a home visit, provided vague or incorrect information as regards the addresses of their relatives, probably hoping they would not be found.

In fact, eighty-seven out of the ninety-seven prisoners seen did agree to one or more relatives or friends being visited. A few made stipulations about which relative might be seen and which might not. In one instance this proved embarrassing, since a particular relative was keen to talk to the social worker but had to be refused because she was black-listed by the prisoner.

Visits were made to one or more informants of eighty-four prisoners. In three cases, although permission was got, visits were not made, in one case (19) because records of home visits were already available, and in two cases no visits were made because the informants could not be traced. In one of these cases (49) the prisoner had supplied false addresses, and in the other (62) the informant, a fellow criminal, proved too difficult to locate and, according to a probation officer's account, was in any event unlikely to co-operate. No relatives were visited in connection with the three prisoners who were not interviewed. The Prison Commissioners' rules forbade visits to the homes of the escaped man or the man who refused an interview, and attempts to trace the relatives of the deceased prisoners proved unsuccessful.

On the whole, the prisoners' relatives were surprisingly co-operative. A few remained unforthcoming, confining themselves to a bare minimum of safe facts (e.g. 7, 14, 20), a few were deliberately deceptive (e.g. 65, 75). In only one instance (45) was the visitor actually turned out of the house, and fortunately in that case other informants were available. Usually she was thanked for the interest shown and the opportunity to discuss problems. In fact, the anxieties shown by some relatives, and their appeals for advice about how they should behave towards the prisoners were sometimes difficult to deal with. In all cases the visitor emphasised that she was not acting in any official capacity, but merely seeking help in the understanding of prisoners' problems. In contrast with the relatives of the intermittent recidivists, who were mostly short-term prisoners, expected home again shortly, the relatives of the preventive detainees were more relaxed and readier to talk at length. They had long since become reconciled to the persistence of the prisoner's criminal habits, and were clear in their minds as to whether or not they wished for further contact with him. They had no immediate problems about what to do when the prisoners were released, for in most cases that was a long time ahead.

3. Social Records

Other sources of information were also used. Each man's prison file was studied. This always contained a list of criminal convictions, giving the nature of the charges on each occasion. It also included the prison medical officer's report of routine physical examination on admission. The men were not given a physical examination for this enquiry, and reliance was placed on the findings on record, supplemented by information supplied by the prisoners themselves. In some instances, old dossiers relating to previous sentences of corrective training were available, and these included psychological assessments and intelligence tests. In the case of the intermittent recidivists, the senior psychologist at Wandsworth, Mr R. S. Taylor, kindly arranged for intelligence testing of any prisoners who had not previously been assessed who seemed mentally dull when interviewed. In the case of the preventive detainees this was not required, since every man had been examined at the allocation centre, and the reports, which were made available to the psychiatrist, invariably included the results of intelligence tests, as well as a personal history and psychological evaluation based upon interviews.

In addition to the prison dossiers, the files at the Criminal Record Office, Scotland Yard, were also consulted, and from these more precise information was obtained about the nature, circumstances and extent of the prisoners' offences, as well as occasional comments on social background, and detailed accounts of employments.

When a prisoner had been recently on probation, or had been in a mental hospital, or had served in the armed forces and was able to supply his reference number, the authorities concerned were asked for their records. In appropriate cases the prisoners were asked to sign a form of consent to the information being made available for the purpose of research. In the case of those preventive detainees[1] who had been to an approved school or Borstal the old records were invariably requested. Unfortunately

[1] In the first series of prisoners, the intermittent recidivists, those who had been to Borstal or approved school were not all asked at interview to specify the names of the institution to which they had been committed, and without this information the records could not be supplied.

most of them had either been destroyed or were reported unobtainable. Of the former, only two reports were found out of twelve, and of the latter only seven out of twenty. This was unfortunate, because such records sometimes contained contemporary reports by social workers describing the offenders' earlier life and family circumstances. In all cases notes from the Central After-Care Association were available, but these provided no details about character or personal life.

4. Discrepant Information

The purpose of the home visits and the examination of old records was to obtain independent information about each prisoner's background and personality. Although some men were surprisingly confiding, in other instances information obtained from elsewhere flatly contradicted the facts of the life story given by the prisoner. In many cases the outside informant gave a different, and usually more unfavourable, picture than that derived from the prison interview. The need to see relatives in order to assess properly an offender's personality was amply confirmed by this experience.

At least half of the men were unreliable in their accounts of themselves. Comparing the findings of this more leisurely investigation with the psychological reports made on preventive detainees at the allocation centre, which were compiled without benefit of information from relatives, one sees how even most shrewd and experienced observers may occasionally be misled, at least on factual details if not on overall assessment. In ten cases, although the general assessment of character was confirmed, individual factual particulars, about employment record or home background, which were quoted in the reports and apparently accepted, proved incorrect. In a further four cases (77, 81, 85, 97) acceptance of the prisoner's untruths affected the conclusions of the reports. In one case, for example (85), the psychologist concluded that the prisoner 'is conscious of the lack of family support and encouragement, and obviously missed the security of a home. He has never had a confidant and has tended to keep things to himself. He has never felt at ease with others and he is awkward socially. . . '. This was contradicted by the evidence of those who knew him outside of prison, who described him as cheerful, very irresponsible and unconcerned, self-confident and able to 'talk his way round anywhere', and not at all shy. The man had given the prison psychologist the impression that his mother was a cold, distant person who had never shown much interest in him. He gave a somewhat different story when interviewed for the purpose of this investigation, mentioning that he recalled his mother giving him food at times when she had none for herself. A visit to the mother confirmed that she was, and always had been, greatly concerned about the prisoner, much to her other sons' disgust. They felt that she had let him take unreasonable advantage of her, but she said firmly that the prisoner was 'her boy' and she would always help him no matter what anyone said.

In order to systematise the collection of data from various sources, and to facilitate subsequent classifications and tabulations, a form was devised, setting out a list of basic points, and as the investigation proceeded a copy of this record form was filled in for each prisoner. The points covered included such matters as age, number of juvenile and adult convictions, classification of offences, latest offence and value of property involved, marital status, children (if any), occupation, father's occupation, grading on work history, grading on sociability, medical and psychiatric diagnoses, intelligence assessment, whether an excessive drinker, whether from a 'broken' home, etc.

Where discrepancies appeared between evidence from different sources, a decision as to the most probably correct version was taken on the merits of each case before making a final entry on the record form. It is worth mentioning at this stage that such decisions are called for frequently in any investigation that makes use of official records. For example, there were occasionaly discrepancies between dates of birth given in prison records and the dates given elsewhere or volunteered by the prisoner. In five instances a date different from that in the prison record was taken as the more probably correct, and this was sometimes important, since the decision might affect the proportion of convictions classed as juvenile. There were also occasional differences in numbers and types of convictions as given in the prison files and the Scotland Yard files. The latter were generally taken as authoritative, and they were used exclusively for statements about value of property involved in offences and similar matters of concern to the police.

III

BACKGROUND OF THE OFFENDERS

1. Criminal Habits

In criminal history and in social background the two groups of prisoners were much alike. At the time of interview, the intermittent recidivists ranged in age from thirty to eighty with an average of forty-four years, and the preventive detainees from thirty-three to sixty-nine with an average of 44·7 years. The average number of convictions[1] was, however, slightly larger among the preventive detainees (13·8 per man as compared with 11·7) and their experience of previous imprisonments was considerably larger (see Table 1, first two columns, also Table 3).

Many of the prisoners, particularly the preventive detainees, had spent a large part of their lives in custody. The sentences of preventive detention ranged from five to ten years, with most men serving either seven or eight years. Eighteen per cent had already served a previous period of preventive detention. Forty-two per cent had been to approved school or Borstal. The time spent at liberty preceding their latest conviction was usually short, less than two years in eighty-six per cent of cases (average 10·9 months, range 0 to 60). In all these respects the intermittent recidivists were not quite so bad. Only twenty-four per cent had been in approved school or Borstal. Their present sentences of imprisonment averaged only two years (range from three months to six years). Their last intervals at liberty were rather longer (less than two years in seventy-five per cent of cases, average 17·9 months, range 0 to 80). However, the differences were not large, and when the criminal records of the fifty intermittent recidivists were examined again, approximately a year after interview, three of them had already become preventive detainees themselves.

Both groups of prisoners were relatively late in starting their (official) criminal careers, with thirty-nine per cent of cases free from any record of convictions as juveniles and a third aged

[1] Throughout the report the number of convictions refers to the number of entries on the criminal record, which gives the number of separate occasions at which an appearance at Court resulted in one or more convictions for criminal offences.

twenty or over before being convicted for the first time (see Table 2). In both groups, the offences for which they had been convicted, both past and present, were mostly offences against property. Offences of physical violence against others were conspicuously few. There were none at all among the charges at the latest convictions of the preventive detainees, and only three (two robberies and a drunken assault) among those of the intermittent recidivists. Judging by the absence of violence in their criminal records, and by the fact that few committed disciplinary offences within the prisons, the preventive detainees in particular appeared an unusually docile group of criminals. Since they have been referred to as including 'a high proportion of difficult and dangerous prisoners, for whom maximum security and close control are essential'[1] it is relevant to summarise the extent of the violent offences in the past histories of this group.

Only eight of the fifty preventive detainees had ever been convicted for violence, none could be considered dangerously aggressive at present, and only one (88) had ever caused serious injury. This man had a conviction for felonious wounding and robbery with violence. He had gone into a jeweller's shop and asked the man in charge to look at a watch. As the man was doing so, he hit him on the head several times with a piece of lead pipe and, while the victim lay unconscious and quite badly injured, he had made off with a lot of watches.

Another preventive detainee had taken part in his youth in a number of armed robberies in America, for which he was twice convicted, but he had not actually injured anybody on those occasions. Another man (98) had one conviction for wounding. He was said to have slashed a prostitute's arm with a razor blade. Another (83) had two convictions for assault, but he was described in records as 'inadequate' rather than aggressive, and was now a certified schizophrenic patient. One prisoner (58) had one conviction for 'demanding money with menaces'. The menaces occurred in a letter to a woman friend in which he threatened to denounce her for immorality. The same individual, when a young man, had once been convicted for non-sexual assaults on two women. On the first of these occasions he had snatched a hat from a woman's head while cycling past. On the other occasion, he had met and accompanied a lady cyclist. After they had journeyed together for some way, she bent down to pump her cycle tyre, and

[1] *Prisons and Borstals*, H.M.S.O., 1957.

he hit her twice — on the head, according to the record — and rode off.

The most puzzling case of all (93) had five convictions for violence and one for rape, although he was described by reliable relatives as ordinarily never quarrelsome or violent. Five of these charges, including the charge of rape, arose from repeated quarrels with his mistress, a lady at least sixteen years older than himself.

Sexual crime played no more than a small part in the criminal histories of either group of prisoners. Charges for sexual offences were included at the latest convictions of five prisoners. These consisted of two preventive detainees convicted for homosexual activities with boys (70, 87), one recidivist convicted for importuning other men (44) another for sexual interference with children (2) and another for incest with his daughters (19). Only five prisoners were sexual recidivists, and three of these were also recidivist offenders against property. Charges for sexual offences occurred in three per cent of the total convictions of all prisoners (see Table 4). None of the sexual offences was accompanied by serious physical violence.

Among the preventive detainees, apart from the two homosexual offenders who were currently convicted of sexual misconduct, a further eight had been so convicted on previous occasions. These included two already mentioned, the man with the somewhat technical rape and assault charges (93) and the aberrant cyclist (58) who had also one conviction for indecent assault. The remainder consisted of one who had had a conviction for living on his wife's earnings as a prostitute (90), one who had interfered with a girl under age (81), one who had been convicted for an act of buggery with his landlady (60), and three with convictions for indecent exposure (63, 96, 99).

In effect, both groups of prisoners consisted almost entirely of persistent thieves, a small minority of whom occasionally committed violent or sexual crimes as well. One important difference between the two groups lay in their method of thieving, the preventive detainees having a much higher proportion of burglars. At their latest conviction, a half of the preventive detainees were charged with breaking and entering or attempting so to do. The intermittent recidivists were more commonly charged with larceny only (see Table 5). In this respect the preventive detainees were the more unusual, since breaking and entering is primarily a young man's province. Another peculiarity of the preventive detainees was the large number of offences which some men had 'taken into consideration' on the occasion of their latest conviction. This sign of reckless persistence in criminal activity was less often found among the intermittent recidivists (see Table 7). These two features probably weigh heavily in the sentencing policy which decides which recidivists go into preventive detention.

The commission of frauds and false pretences constituted an important minority of the crimes against property. These ranged from attempts to defraud the Post Office by altering savings account books, through selling goods obtained on hire purchase, to the extortion of large sums by plausible misrepresentations. Twelve of the preventive detainees and three of the intermittent recidivists were habitual 'false pretenders' (that is, the majority of their convictions included one or more charges of fraud or false pretences). These fifteen prisoners were particularly late starters in crime, only one of them (94) had been convicted as a juvenile.

Contrary to what one might expect, both groups of prisoners, but especially the preventive detainees, included a substantial proportion of habitually petty thieves and very few enterprising swindlers on the grand scale. Most of their crimes seemed to have been undertaken for the sake of rather trivial loot, and carried out without previous organisation or planning and without the aid of accomplices. Where the values of property involved in the main charges at the latest conviction were known, they did not exceed ten pounds in a third of the preventive detainees and a quarter of the intermittent recidivists (see Table 6). Owing to the high frequency of offences among the preventive detainees, although each individual incident was generally petty, the aggregate of offences 'taken into consideration' sometimes involved very substantial sums. Ten men had between them 855 cases taken into consideration at their latest conviction, the property involved amounting to a total value of over eight thousand pounds (see Table 7).

2. Social Antecedents

In social origin, the hundred prisoners were by no means limited to the lower strata of the working class. The occupations of their fathers or guardians were specified in most cases, and a half of these fell into the category of definable trades or semi-skilled jobs, such as carpenter, miner, salesman, cook or regular soldier. Just over a quarter were unskilled manual workers. The remainder were possessed of special knowledge or training and included eight who ran their own businesses and nine who belonged to managerial, executive or professional grades.

The prisoners themselves had fallen in socio-economic status compared with their fathers. Graded according to their customary employment, or longest period of employment, the majority were unskilled men, mostly casual labourers. The fathers of the intermittent recidivists and the preventive detainees were similar in the range of their occupations, but of the two groups of prisoners the preventive detainees had sunk lower (see Table 8).

The falling away in work performance compared with their fathers was not due to low intelligence, since this was not a feature of the group. All of the preventive detainees had been tested at the allocation centre, and their average intelligence quotient was 99·1, with a range of variability from 70, which is mildly defective (64) to 135, which is bright enough for any profession (56), but the majority had close to average values between 91 and 109 (see Table 9). Among the intermittent recidivists, all those suspected of dullness were tested, but only three had intelligence quotients of less than 80. Some of the prisoners appeared at interview to be very dull, but this was due to apathy and ineffectiveness in social communication more often than to actual intellectual deficiency.

Most of the prisoners came of hard-working, respectable parents. Only four per cent (including two preventive detainees) had a parent with a record of criminal convictions, although seventeen per cent (including nine preventive detainees) had either a parent or brother with a record. The total number of known brothers or half-brothers of the hundred prisoners amounted to 183 of whom 23 (12·6 per cent) were known to have had convictions. The great majority of these brothers were not merely non-criminal, but actually in satisfactory employment and behaving as responsible fathers of families and generally useful citizens. This contrast was frequently remarked upon by the prisoners, who time and time again described themselves as the only black sheep in the family.

The association between broken homes and subsequent criminality has been so often pointed out that it was no surprise to discover that a half of the prisoners had experienced prolonged or permanent separation from one or both natural parents before reaching the age of fifteen. Broken homes, as here defined in terms of the absence of a natural parent, did not necessarily coincide with unsatisfactory upbringing. In some cases a missing parent was replaced by conscientious and affectionate relatives, step-parents or foster parents.

In eight cases absence of one parent was due to desertion or marital separations, but more commonly it was the result of a bereavement. Twenty per cent of the prisoners had lost a father, eight per cent had lost a mother, and a further two per cent had lost both. This incidence of orphanhood, thirty per cent having lost one or both parents before fifteen, is distinctly larger than would be expected of a random sample of the population.[1]

Eleven prisoners had been fostered or adopted, or had spent at least a part of their childhood in institutions, on account of illegitimacy or orphanhood. A further six had been in residential schools for other reasons, usually on account of problem behaviour with which the parents were unable or unwilling to cope.

Vulnerability to delinquency has been said to vary with the number of children in the family (those from large families being more delinquent-prone) and also with the position of the child in order of birth (the eldest and youngest of a family running a special risk). Table 10 shows the numbers of prisoners from different sizes of family. The proportion of only children is not unusual, but the proportion from large families is rather large even in comparison with that reported in connection with juvenile delinquents (see Table 10a). The numbers occupying either eldest or youngest positions, as opposed to intermediate positions, is just about what might be expected from chance, when family sizes are taken into account.[2]

3. Comparisons with other Groups of Prisoners

In spite of the intermittent recidivists being a specially selected group, the findings throughout the present enquiry suggest that they have much in common with the preventive detainees. All of the characteristics mentioned so far, including such points as

[1] The corresponding figure in the 1921 census was 16·6 per cent. In a recent survey of patients attending general practitioners in Hampstead it was 19·6 per cent. See: Brown, F., 'Depression and Childhood Bereavement', *Journ. Mental Science*, 1961, 107, 754–77.

[2] See: Miller, E., 'The Problem of Birth Order and Delinquency', *English Studies in Criminal Science*, 1949, 2, 227–39; Lees, J. P. *et al.*, 'Family or Sibship Position and Some Aspects of Juvenile Delinquency', *Brit. Journ. Delinquency*, 1954, 5, 46–65; Sletto, R. F., 'Sibling Position and Juvenile Delinquency', *American Journ. Sociology*, 1934, 39, 657–69.

intelligence range, age range, social background, type and scale of offences, and age range at first convictions, apply in some degree to both groups. The chief differences lie in those trends indicative of severity of maladjustment, personal and social, which, though present in both groups of prisoners, are obviously more extreme in the case of the preventive detainees. This is reflected in such indices as frequency of offences and poor work record and service record, as well as in incidence of personality deviation and mental illness. These contrasts will become more obvious in later sections of this report. The differences are almost invariably in the same direction, and suggest that the preventive detainee group exhibits in extreme form the trends apparent to a lesser degree among the group of somewhat less habitual prisoners. In other words, the psycho-social trends march in unison with the frequency of criminal convictions. This generalisation is worth keeping in mind when looking at the results presented in subsequent sections.

The group of preventive detainees surveyed in this enquiry, although small, is probably fairly representative of preventive detainees in general. Comparable figures are available, as regards criminal histories and certain social data, in the results of two other recent surveys of unselected groups of preventive detainees. The first, by R. S. Taylor, Senior Psychologist at H.M. Prison, Wandsworth,[1] was based upon interview data and penal records from one hundred consecutive admissions to the allocation centre for preventive detainees at Wandsworth, in the year 1956. The second survey,[2] by W. H. Hammond and Edna Greenburg, was a Home Office Research Unit project based upon penal records, and in particular upon the After-trial Calendars, concerning the 178 men sentenced to preventive detention in 1956, as well as those liable to preventive detention but not so sentenced. The groups of detainees covered in Taylor's and Hammond's investigations overlapped to a negligible extent.

The present findings agree with both of the earlier surveys in regard to the preponderance of unskilled labourers (see Table 8), the high proportion of house-breakers, the small sums involved in many of the offences against property, the scarcity of seriously violent offenders, and the somewhat high average age on first conviction (see Tables 1, 5). The present findings also agree with Taylor's results in regard to the small number from criminal

[1] Taylor, R. S., 'The Habitual Criminal', *Brit. Journ. Criminol.*, 1960, 1, 21–36.

[2] *The Persistent Offender*, H.M.S.O., in the press.

families, the substantial proportion who come from incomplete or broken homes and in the absence of any conspicuous deviation from the normal intelligence range (see Table 9). The high incidence of unmarried men and of social isolates, a matter commented upon in the next section, is another point upon which the present findings agree with Taylor's results (see Table 11). The present sample is perhaps slightly untypical in that average age on committal to detention and average number of previous convictions are both slightly lower than expected. There seems little doubt, however, that the group adequately reflects the important trends. This consideration becomes crucial when dealing with psychiatric peculiarities not covered by previous investigations in regard to which no immediate check upon the adequacy of the sample is available. The fact that the group has proved satisfactorily representative on other points increases the probability that the psychiatric findings also are fairly representative of preventive detainees in general.

IV

DEVIATIONS OF PERSONALITY

1. The Extent of Social-Maladjustment

Some persistent thieves behave conventionally in other respects, ply their dishonest trade diligently, in fact appear to be normal, mature personalities. Most of the prisoners studied in this enquiry, however, seemed woefully lacking in ability to fulfil ordinary social expectations in any sphere of life.

Their disability was most obvious in personal relationships. Among the preventive detainees, a half had never married (although the average age of the group was nearly forty), and only eight per cent were actually living with wives at the time of their latest arrest (see Table 11). The intermittent recidivists were rather better in this respect, with twenty-six per cent unmarried and thirty-two per cent living with wives, although at least twelve per cent were on very uncertain terms and likely before long to become separated or divorced. Their marital disputes and separations were more often due to temperamental incompatibility than to the wives' reactions to their thieving habits. Their peculiarities had a noticeable affect upon their reproduction rate. So far as was known, the fifty preventive detainees had no more than thirty-eight children; the intermittent recidivists had seventy-six children.

Evidence of long-standing social isolation was especially obvious among the preventive detainees. Although a minoritywere adept at short-lived contacts for purposes of exploitation, few had any permanent friendships, seventy-two per cent were living alone at the time of their arrest, and about a half suffered from undue diffidence or shyness. Study of individual case histories showed that this social awkwardness and isolation had always been present, and could not be wholly attributed to rejection by society on account of criminal convictions. A similar, though less extreme, trend was obvious among the intermittent recidivists, thirty per cent of whom were considered solitary or socially withdrawn to an unusual degree.

A general lack of loyalty was reflected in appallingly bad work records. The relative absence of special skills or training among the prisoners represented but one facet of a general reluctance to submit to a regular work routine, and an inability to settle in any place for long. Only twelve per cent were reported to have been satisfactory employees during their more recent periods at liberty, the remainder having frequent, unexplained changes of job or long periods without recognisable employment. The preventive detainees were particularly bad in this respect. According to police reports, forty per cent of them had never stayed in one place of employment for more than three months in the whole of their lives. Although many of them complained of being discriminated against by employers on account of their criminal record, they seemed able to find jobs but not to keep them. Usually they were said to have 'left of their own accord' or been dismissed for absenteeism rather than for incompetence. At interview the prisoners often gave the discovery of their criminal record as a reason for leaving jobs, but in most cases difficulty in conforming to requirements at work had been present before their criminality became established. There was, however, a twenty per cent minority (including twelve of the preventive detainees) who had apparently worked satisfactorily at first but deteriorated in later years.

One might have expected these difficult characters to have done better in the more controlled setting of military service. Actually, out of eighty prisoners known to have been in the armed forces, no more than eleven (including only one of the preventive detainees) completed their periods of service without getting into trouble with the authorities. Even among these eleven, four had been discharged prematurely on medical grounds. All the others deserted or went absent repeatedly, or were discharged with unsatisfactory characters, or spent long periods in detention, or else were convicted of criminal offences by the civilian courts. It would seem that the majority were incapable of adapting to military life. In fact, eleven were discharged on psychiatric recommendations.[1]

Yet another indication of social malaise was the prevalence of excessive drinking, which amounted to a serious problem in the

[1] In marked contrast to their reactions to service life, few caused any trouble during their preventive detention. They generally kept to the rules and did not appear on disciplinary charges. In most cases their service in the forces had taken place many years previously, and in the meantime they may well have grown more docile, or perhaps more institutionalised.

lives of at least twenty per cent of the preventive detainees and forty per cent of the Wandsworth recidivists. In some instances there was an obvious association between getting drunk and then committing offences recklessly, or between periods of heavy drinking and simultaneous thieving in order to pay for it. Some relatives complained that prisoners had neglected their social obligations in order to go off on drinking sprees. In spite of all this, hardly any of the prisoners were severely addicted, in the sense that they never had periods of relative sobriety when out of prison. None of them complained about feeling particularly deprived on account of absence of alcohol during their imprisonments. The majority appeared to be periodic drinkers of the 'symptomatic' type, that is men inclined to resort to the bottle as a tension-relieving process. With the single exception of a man (16) who had been admitted to an observation ward suffering from an alcoholic delusional psychosis, none of the prisoners had been under treatment for alcoholism or were diagnosed as suffering from the physical diseases which result from persistent alcoholic excesses.

Of the two most serious instances of alcoholic tendency among the preventive detainees, one was a severe periodic drinker (66) who was in the habit of calling upon old ladies, pretending to represent a firm of opticians, and collecting money for non-existent spectacles. He would immediately squander the proceeds in the pub, and then call on other potential victims, still smelling of drink. His own version was that he turned to drink when he felt ill or worried, sitting in the pub taking glasses of whisky one after the other. Then he would go out and 'get into trouble'. 'I always drink beforehand,' he said. The other instance of a particularly severe drinking problem (71) was a man who had been consuming beer heavily from an early age. He first got into the habit through performing in public houses as a singer. He had several convictions for assaulting the police when drunk. He admitted to being completely 'adrift' in recent years, that is wandering about in a drunken state, attempting to break into premises, and being frequently caught doing so.

In the next section, which deals with psychiatric symptoms, it is shown that a substantial minority of prisoners were suffering from mental illness of either the psychotic or neurotic variety. This fact, however, does not explain the social disturbance which nearly all of them displayed. Their neurotic symptoms were not of crippling severity and were insufficient to account for their gross maladjustment. In all instances of psychotic breakdown, the men had been serious social misfits long before symptoms of mental illness appeared. In other words, in spite of the superimposed mental symptoms which were present in some individuals, the fundamental difficulty in nearly all cases was an underlying defect or immaturity of personality.

A plethora of words such as psychopath, sociopath, defective ego, constitutional inferiority, and social immaturity have been used by psychiatrists to describe this condition. The term personality deviant is perhaps the best, since it is descriptive without implying any particular theory. All of the prisoners in this survey were classified into normals or deviants, using inability to form satisfactory relationships with others as the main criterion of deviance, but also taking into consideration evidence of impulsiveness and reckless disregard of consequences. Since some men had apparently changed in personality with age, the assessment was made on their history after the age of thirty, and before the onset of illness in the case of the psychotics. Only those showing considerable limitations in many aspects of personality were classed as deviants, but even so all but eight per cent of the preventive detainees and sixteen per cent of the intermittent recidivists were diagnosed as personality deviants. The following two examples, both preventive detainees, illustrate the standards used in the assessment of personality deviation, which is, after all, a matter of degree and not a hard and fast diagnosis.

The first was classed as a non-deviant:

Case 65

A married man, aged thirty-nine, with fourteen convictions for offences against property and one for repeated absconding from an approved school. He was a skilled burglar, whose enterprises were well planned and carried out with the aid of accomplices. He arranged alibis and utilised professional receivers. The proceeds of his crimes amounted to many thousands of pounds with which he was able to afford large cars and other luxuries.

The pattern showed early. At the age of fourteen he ran away from a poverty-stricken home in the company of some 'flashy' friends. Six months later a comment in a Borstal report read: 'A lad of initiative and ambition. He has got through a lot of money and found it very easy to steal.' A year later a medical report described him as 'Of bold, adventurous disposition. He is aggressive, self-reliant and resourceful.

He has shown keen gambling instincts, and this, coupled with bad associates, and abundance of energy and a desire for excitement, have led him into trouble. . . .' He had two younger brothers both of whom followed rather similar criminal careers. Twenty-two years later, the psychologist's report at the allocation centre read: 'It would seem that he has been unable to find a socially acceptable outlet for his abilities and energies, and has canalised these into crime and gambling.'

In spite of his bad record, the prisoner maintained a polite, cheerful attitude when seen for this enquiry. As observers had previously remarked, he was a man with likeable qualities. He was firmly attached to his family. He was still in touch with his ageing father, a hard-working, respectable man, who lamented his son's thieving, but commented that he had always told the truth and never pretended to be other than a thief. The prisoner had been married twice. His first wife left him taking their child with her during one of his periods of imprisonment. This upset him greatly as he had been very fond of them, and he did all he could to get them back. He was also firmly attached to his second wife, and to the son she bore him, and by all appearances he had seen to it that they were well provided with money. His second wife was an attractive woman of beguiling manner and to all appearances a good mother, although formerly a professional prostitute and still an active criminal.

This case provided a fair example of the so-called 'socialised criminal', a man who rejects some of the standards of the law-abiding community as regards property rights, but remains warm-hearted and capable of normal human relationships among his own group of fellow criminals.

The next example is that of an all-round misfit who was unhesitatingly diagnosed as deviant:

Case 72

A single man, aged forty-six, with repeated convictions for petty thieving. For many years he had led an unsettled, almost tramp-like existence, and was on record as of 'no fixed abode'. Although a satisfactory worker while in employment, he was apt to become upset at minor frustrations and wander off aimlessly, breaking into unoccupied houses to sleep, and then making off with any small amounts of cash or articles that happened to be lying around.

He came of an unfortunate background. His father, a former sergeant major in the regular army, was a stern and irritable man who suffered from duodenal ulcers and asthma. As the most timorous of the children he came in for the brunt of the father's temper. His mother was a strong-minded and not very maternal character. During his infancy she was working at three jobs simultaneously and not arriving home until 10 p.m. At the age of seven he was sent away to a residential school on account of persistent wandering from home and truancy, and thereafter he spent the larger part of his life in institutions.

At the age of eleven he fell from a window at his residential school, and then said he was trying to kill himself in order to escape harsh punishments. He was therefore admitted to a mental hospital, where he was noticed to have a slight stutter, and to be somewhat sulky and disobedient, but no mental abnormality was found. He was questioned by Cyril (later Sir Cyril) Burt, who concluded that he was a mischievous liar.

At the interview for this enquiry, he looked older than his age, and had a soft, effeminate manner. He spoke with a pronounced lisp, and was almost pathetically compliant in signing consent forms and agreeing to enquiries about his relatives, with whom he had long since lost touch. He confessed to having no sexual feelings for women, and to having practised passive homosexuality and transvestitism all his life. He was not without shame about this, remarking that he would kill himself rather than stand trial for homosexuality and hear his sexual habits described in public. He had once been discovered by the police asleep in an empty house dressed up in women's clothes, but he had never been charged with a sexual offence.

As the interview drew to a close the prisoner expressed very clearly his yearning to dependency. 'As far as I can see there's nothing for me in the future unless I can get someone really interested. I seem to flop if left to myself. I always have to have somebody saying "come on we'll do this, or come we'll do that".'

2. Types of Deviance

The men classed as personality deviants were further subdivided, according to a modification of the system first introduced by Sir David Henderson, into the predominantly passive inadequate and the predominantly active-aggressive.

Both sub-types have in common a generalised instability, a failure to cope with ordinary frustrations, but whereas the aggressives respond by hitting back at the environment, the inadequates tend to collapse into passive resistance and querulous dependency. Inadequates tend to be typically feckless people, grossly lacking in drive and initiative. They are always complaining and demanding help from authorities, without exerting any effort themselves. They tend to form one-sided, parasitic relationships with whoever will put up with them. They never seem able to fend for themselves. Their spinelessness and sloth suggest that they have found social demands too much for them, and have contracted out of the system altogether, so that they no longer bother to try to do the things expected of a normal citizen. Henderson[1] describes them as 'facile individuals who follow the path of least resistance. . . . It is only after they have failed their friends repeatedly and have shown an almost entire absence of warmth and honour that they are recognised as suffering from an essential lack, an inability to meet life fairly. . . . They accept everything and give nothing in return.'

In contrast to the spineless inadequates, the aggressives are more actively defiant and rebellious, and altogether more energetic and resourceful, but their energies are misdirected. Henderson is inclined to limit the term to those with tendencies towards actual violence, of an unrestrained impulsive kind, but for present purposes all those with overtly predatory and actively anti-social attitudes are included,[2] regardless of a history of physical violence, which was in any event infrequent among these prisoners. The present classification follows Norman Cameron's concept of the 'inept social deviant'.[3] The inadequate is so immature he has never started to learn to perform social roles effectively, so he tends to be a solitary, non-participant, but the active deviant really does take part, albeit in an inept or inappropriate fashion. He can seem, for short periods, a charming companion or a model prisoner, but it is as if he were playing an imitative role rather than living up to real adult responsibilities.

The sub-division of personality deviants according to an aggressivity-passivity criterion has proved useful in many clinical studies. In a recent discussion of passive inadequates, De Berker[4] points out that their prevalence among recidivists in prison greatly exceeds that of the more spectacular aggressives, who attract the label psychopath, and receive an unfair share of attention on account of their obstreperous and difficult behaviour. By means of a factor analysis based on the recorded characteristics of prisoners at Wakefield, Marcus[5] has produced some scientific evidence that

[1] Henderson, D. K., *Psychopathic Personalities*, London, 1939.

[2] Again, this usage differs from Henderson's in that his includes active deceivers and confidence tricksters among the passive category. See: 'Psychopathic Constitution and Criminal Behaviour', *English Studies in Criminal Science*, 1949, 2, 105–21.

[3] Cameron, N. and Margaret A., *Behaviour Pathology*, Boston, 1951.

[4] De Berker, P., 'State of Mind Reports: The Inadequate Personality', *Brit. Journ. Criminol.*, 1960, 1, 6–20.

[5] Marcus, B., 'A Dimensional Study of a Prison Population', *Brit. Journ. Criminol.*, 1960, 1, 130–53.

offenders fall naturally into types according to the dominance of either of the opposing qualities of aggressivity or passivity. He found that the characteristics of individual prisoners could be ranged along a natural scale of variation, with out-going — expansive — aggressive types, at one extreme, and timorous — seclusive — inadequate types at the other extreme. Those at the inadequate end of the scale had a predilection for petty thieving and homosexual offences, and had often spent a large part of their lives in penal institutions. Those at the aggressive end of the scale tended to commit heterosexual assaults, frauds, and false pretences, and had often come from openly rejecting parental homes. He summed up as follows: 'It seems as if there are two ways of being anti-social — to hit out . . . or to drift along with a spineless disregard for responsibilities.'

If it is true that both passive-inadequate and active-aggressive types of deviant represent maldevelopments of personality, then the inadequates would seem to be the more abnormal. Henderson[1] comments that, 'The inadequate groups are almost more consistently abnormal or immoral, more malignantly involved in their individual tendency.' They let all opportunities slide and default by neglect. When they take to crime they do so *faute de mieux* more often than by deliberate choice. The aggressives, however, as De Berker points out, show 'a certain exuberance and a certain determination in the pursuit of . . . short-term goals'. Nevertheless, the expansive and temporarily successful false pretender, though not without a certain roguish charm and superficial bonhomie, is often almost as abortive and unsatisfactory in his more intimate personal relationships as the inadequate.

Among the prisoners surveyed in this enquiry, the difference between the passive-inadequate and the active-aggressive types was reflected in their respective attitudes to offences. The inadequate generally described their offences as the consequence of finding themselves in a difficult situation, such as being out of work, or being let down by someone. It was when they were feeling generally fed-up and helpless that they were apt, on the spur of the moment, and almost always when alone, to commit some stupid and usually petty theft. The inadequates often claimed that their offences were forced upon them by misery or desperation, although to the detached onlooker it might seem that they were simply choosing an easy way out of a difficulty.

[1] Henderson, D. K., *Psychopathic Personalities*, London, 1939, p. 68.

These passively motivated offences form a complete contrast to the deliberately anti-social acts of the active-aggressive deviants. Active crimes tend to be purposeful, thought out in advance, and embarked upon, often with the aid of accomplices, in a deliberate effort to wrest some prize from the law-abiding community. Sometimes considerable energy and initiative goes into these activities, and the criminals, when questioned, not uncommonly admit a feeling of enjoyment and satisfaction. Such criminals hardly ever say that they were forced into their offences, but they often attempt to justify themselves by denying culpability, by claiming that they only steal from the rich or the well-insured, or by saying that crime is the only means open to them of achieving a good standard of living.

Actively anti-social motivation characterised the offences of both the active-aggressive personality deviants and the non-deviants. The only obvious difference was that the crimes carried out by relatively normal individuals were on the whole better organised and directed to a specific prize, where the deviants went in for more diffusely anti-social behaviour.

Although the concept of active or passive deviancy, like that of deviancy itself, is a matter of degree, and a few cases were to neither one extreme or the other, it was still possible to classify each deviant prisoner according to his predominant characteristics. The inadequates formed the majority (fifty-two per cent). They were especially prevalent among the preventive detainees (fifty-eight per cent).

The following examples, the second taken from the preventive detainee group and the first from the intermittent recidivists, illustrate the differences between the two types of deviant.

Case 7

A married man of forty-six, separated from his wife and intermittently cohabiting with another woman by whom he had a son of thirteen. He was convicted on eight occasions, all for offences against property. His cohabitee was interviewed, but gave hardly any information, repeatedly insisting that 'He's nothing to do with me dear,' or 'I wouldn't know anything about that, love.' The prisoner's story was therefore largely unconfirmed.

The prisoner was a healthy man of wiry build, garrulous and plausible at interview, but reluctant to admit to anything not already known in his record. He showed no apparent tension or guilt, adopted a cheerful, 'couldn't-care-less' attitude to his present imprisonment and was even rather proud of his criminal exploits, although ready to admit that he was irresponsible over gambling, and that one of his convictions was the result of trying to steal while drunk. As a rule, he said, he was not an excessive drinker. He was sexually promiscuous, however, and had had several attacks of venereal disease. According to his cohabitee, he had been evicted for taking back to his room many different girls of all ages.

The prisoner came of respectable working-class parents, and had one younger brother who was a hard-working family man. His father, a former regular soldier, was a strict disciplinarian, but the prisoner was, by his own account, a stubborn character who 'wouldn't be put upon' and 'wouldn't knuckle down to father'. His schooldays were uneventful. He mixed easily and liked sports. He trained as an electrician, but gave it up in favour of work on amusement fairs. Then he joined the army and while serving was convicted, together with some other young men, of breaking and entering. He maintained that his father was responsible for his first prison sentence, having told the Court, 'I can't help him, he's out of control.'

A year after his release he was convicted again for a similar offence and sent to Borstal. He escaped and committed further offences. He was persuaded by his mother to give himself up. At the age of twenty-four he met and married an orphan girl. He complained that she proved to be a neglectful mother and an unfaithful wife. 'So I just left her and she had the children put in a home. Now she has about six more kids — all colours.' For the next seven years, he worked steadily as an electrician in an aircraft factory and stayed there as a reserved employee throughout the war.[1] He finally left, on a false plea of ill-health, because he wanted to set up on his own as a street trader. Apart from an offence of selling elastic above price, he remained conviction-free for a further ten years. 'I was always able to make money. I've always known how to get money for a car without being caught, but I never bothered to try to do anything.' About his relapse into crime he said he was persuaded by some friends to join with them in a house-breaking expedition. 'I'm an easy-going type — love anybody. It's stupid. I only get caught through going in with others. Sooner or later one will get caught and talk. So I just let myself get caught before that happens. I'm not stupid.' He was in fact simultaneously convicted for fraud, having gambled away money given to him for the purchase of a television.

This man was considered a personality deviant on account of his short-lived, fleeting personal relationships, his chronically unsettled, drifting way of life, and his unrealistic and asocial attitudes. He had too much initiative and self-sufficiency to be classed as 'inadequate',

[1] This point was confirmed, and this man was among those considered to have had a genuine interlude of relative honesty.

and was accordingly placed in the group of active-aggressive deviants, although there was no evidence that he was prone to physical violence.

Case 55

A single man aged thirty-five, classified as a passive-inadequate personality-deviant. An old Borstal report described him as 'a poor, miserable type' and 'a body without a spirit'. The Royal Navy discharged him as mentally retarded, although, on testing at the allocation centre, his intelligence quotient worked out at just about average. His elder sister said that even as a boy he was solitary and unfriendly, generally lazy, neglectful of his appearance, not interested in anything, and without affection even for his own family. He was always restless and irresponsible, quite unconcerned when caught by the police, and didn't seem to mind living in penal institutions. He had eleven convictions, three of them including offences of arson.

The events which led to his present imprisonment started with the theft of a letter containing money which had been delivered at the hostel where he was staying temporarily. He went away with the money, hoping he said, to find a job in a neighbouring town. Failing to do so, he presented himself at the door of a mental hospital and asked for treatment. He was refused admission, whereupon he set fire to a hay stack.

At interview, his account of his motives for these offences ran as follows: 'When a man has no money and nowhere to go he's not going to let himself starve. Landladies always want a week's cash in advance. If he can't get taken into lodgings then he puts himself out to get somewhere. He'll put himself out to commit some sort of crime, setting fire, breaking a window or something. Not that he's mental. He does it out of deliberation. Whatever you do you get sent to prison.' Asked how he felt while committing the offences he replied: 'I feel annoyed at myself and at other people. I seem to have failed myself and to have failed other people.'

He talked to the psychiatrist at great length, complaining repeatedly that no one had ever taken an interest in him. 'I'm the sort that people don't want to know. It has always been like that.' He stated that he suffered from dreadful moods, which lasted days at a time, but added 'I'd never get around to killing myself. I haven't got the guts.' Asked about plans for the future he said 'I've given up thinking about it'. About women he stated in a resentful tone that he had no time for them, and would never chase after them because they were generally stuck up and not interested 'in the likes of me'.

He was full of complaints about neglect. 'I can't see any hope for myself. They don't give you a proper trade.' 'If you report sick the doctors think you are a malingerer. They don't impress me anyway. They're not interested in us.' His final remarks were to the effect that there must be something wrong with him and he ought to have a transfer to a mental hospital.

Other examples of personality deviants quoted elsewhere in the report include cases 1, 6, 72 (pages 35, 44, 24), which were classed as inadequates, and cases 5, 8 (pages 38, 49), which were classed as aggressives.

3. Contrasts between Passive and Active Deviants

This classification of prisoners into active deviants, passive deviants and non-deviants was made subjectively on the basis of the total impression of the man's history and attitudes gained from interviewing him and considering the evidence of outside informants. When the groups so classified were later compared systematically according to various objective criteria, such as marital status, service and employment record, scope and frequency and type of crime, and also the scores achieved on psychological tests, consistent differences appeared on all counts. It would seem, therefore, that the method of classification serves to identify certain dominant trends, or clusters of characteristics, which have relevance to many aspects of behaviour. For example, nearly all of the prisoners classed as solitary individuals, the great majority of the unmarried, and most of those with obvious psychiatric symptoms, came from the passive-inadequate group (see Table 12). The inadequates also included a high proportion of men with records of more than ten convictions. The non-deviants, on the other hand, were characterised by the relatively high proportion who had had satisfactory periods of employment or of military service and were living amicably with their wives. In these respects, the active-aggressive group occupied an intermediate position.

The type and scope of offences varied most markedly between the different personality groupings. The inadequates were mostly responsible for offences on a small scale. The value of property concerned in the main charges at the latest conviction (or at the latest conviction to which a value could be applied) did not exceed fifty pounds in sixty-eight per cent of the inadequates compared with forty-seven per cent of the aggressives and only thirty-three per cent of the non-deviants (see Table 13). The more enterprising offences were most often committed by the non-deviants, to a lesser degree by the aggressives, and rarely by the inadequates. Thus, most of those whose latest offences concerned the largest amounts came from the small group of a dozen non-deviants and none at all came from the large group of inadequates (see Table 14). The inadequates also included fewer habitual false pretenders. The intermittent recidivists were responsible for a greater number of large-scale offences than the preventive detainees, but they also included a larger number of non-deviant personalities.

By and large the scale of offences remained surprisingly constant for each individual, the inadequate keeping to petty offences all their lives, the more enterprising criminals commencing their substantial depredations of property early in their criminal careers. A minority, however, had undoubtedly adopted increasingly ambitious criminal goals. Among the preventive detainees were seven men whose recent offences, gauged by the value of property concerned, had at least doubled in size in recent years.[1] None of these men appeared among the inadequate group. It would seem that the inadequates remain permanently ineffective and incapable of profiting by experience even in the realm of criminal activity.

A similar comparison between recent and past offences was made, but including the total value of property concerned in all the offences taken into consideration on each occasion of conviction. On this basis a considerably larger proportion of prisoners, including some of the inadequates, appeared to have increased their offences. It is true, therefore, that some inadequates become a worse menace to property as their experience increases, but in their case it is because their offences become more frequent while remaining in each instance relatively slight.

It might be argued that the so-called inadequates are simply the less intelligent of the criminal group. The results of the intelligence tests which we applied to the preventive detainees by the prison psychologists did show an association. The mean intelligence quotient for the whole group of fifty was 99·1, but for the twenty-nine inadequates it was four points less — 95·3 — and for the

[1] The figure was calculated as follows: (1) Take property values associated with main charges at each conviction. (2) Exclude individuals for whom values never exceed £50. (3) In each case remaining average the latest three recorded values. (4) For each individual separately compare this average with values recorded at previous convictions. (5) For seven individuals the recent average was at least double any previously recorded value.

twenty-one others correspondingly more — 104·5. Even so, intelligence was clearly by no means the whole story. A third of the inadequates were above average in intelligence and a third of the remainder were below average. The inadequate group included six active psychotics whose scores may have been depressed by illness. Furthermore, the apathy and fatal despondency with which the inadequates approached every task, intelligence tests included, may well have hindered their performance.

V

INTERLUDES OF HONESTY

1. Genuine and Pseudo Gaps in Penal Records

As previously described (see page 3), the first series of prisoners was specially selected on account of interesting gaps in their records of convictions, the meaning of which was obscure. Table 15 sets out for each of the fifty cases the intervals at liberty between convictions arranged in chronological sequence from left to right. On scanning these figures some interesting points emerged.

In spite of having included only those with at least one conviction-free interval of four years or more, such long intervals were the exception. Most prisoners did not have more than the one substantial interval which had caused them to be selected. The majority of intervals did not exceed one year. Therefore, although the group has been referred to as intermittent, the intermissions were exceptional rather than regular. However, when a substantial interval did occur it was as likely to be very long, say over six years, as moderately long, that is between three and six years (see Table 16). This fact suggests that the more substantial intervals constitute a different phenomenon from the general run of shorter intervals, and if this is so it seems plausible to seek for special circumstances or special causes associated with them.

The first task was to try to sort out those gaps corresponding with a genuine interlude of honesty from those due simply to successful evasion. Certainty being unattainable, the following criteria were used. Since the existence of an unusual gap in the record provided *prima facie* evidence for a change in behaviour, all gaps were classed as genuine except in any one of the following circumstances.

1. The prisoner himself confessed to offences committed at such times that it was evident that he had never had a full four years' gap. This excluded nine cases.
2. Evidence from relatives or social reports contradicted the prisoner's claim to have had at least one crime-free gap. This excluded five cases.

3. Scrutiny of files at the Criminal Record Office, Scotland Yard, showed that the prisoner was known to have, or was very strongly suspected of having, committed offences at times which effectively cancelled his claim to a four-year period of honesty. This excluded a further six cases, but these were all cases which on other grounds seemed suspect or implausible. In all, thirty out of fifty prisoners[1] were finally classed as having had at least one genuine gap during which, if not completely honest, they were at least much less criminal than usual.

The following two examples illustrate the use of the criteria for deciding whether to count a prisoner as having had a 'genuine' gap of at least four years of honesty:

Case 1

A single man aged fifty-seven who was first convicted at the age of twenty-five. From then until the age of thirty-four he had a total of nine convictions and nine terms of imprisonment. After that and until the age of forty-six, he was at liberty for twelve years without any conviction. Subsequently, he had twenty-one further convictions with sentences of imprisonment totalling twelve years two months. In his last eleven years he had spent substantially more time in prison than at liberty, and had not had more than a few months at a time outside prison.

His offences were breaking in, stealing, wilful damage and insulting behaviour. In later years his offences were almost exclusively 'wilful damage', which consisted of breaking windows of shops, telephone kiosks, and the like. He said that sometimes he broke windows for the purpose of taking something from a shop display, but sometimes he did it because he felt fed up or because he wanted to get back to prison for the sake of food and shelter. He said he once smashed a telephone kiosk glass in temper because he couldn't manage to extract any coppers from the machine. On one occasion recently, when he was feeling particularly fed up, he picked up a broom in a public convenience and smashed a mirror with it. Then he waited while the attendant went to fetch the police. In Court the police stated he was depressed at the time of his offence.

[1] It will be recalled that it was at the outset decided to consider only gaps in established criminal careers and therefore to count only those both preceded and followed by at least two convictions in adult courts. For this reason, no account has been taken in the discussion of intervals at liberty immediately following the first adult conviction or immediately preceding the latest conviction. Had these intervals been taken into account they would have served to add only one case (40) to the group with a genuine crime-free period.

When he was about ten years old his quarrelsome, drunken father deserted the home and thereafter he spent the remainder of his childhood, up to the age of fifteen, together with his brother, in a local authority residential school. After finishing at a sea-training school, he went to sea in the merchant navy from the age of fifteen to seventeen. He left on impulse, but was unable to find work ashore and joined the army at the age of eighteen. He served a year and was then discharged as he could not pass a test. At the age of nineteen he went into the navy and served satisfactorily as a stoker for five years. He left because, he said, he got fed up and felt like a change, and again tried to get work ashore. His relatives would not accommodate him, so he had to live in hostels. He found difficulty in obtaining work, so he started breaking into shops and stealing money. He was caught and convicted for the first time after about a year. He was then aged twenty-five. Thereafter he was in and out of prison for the rest of his life. Each time he was released he felt helpless and soon lapsed into thieving.

His long conviction-free period began at the age of thirty-four. He said that at that time he found a place in a comfortable local authority hostel where he was allowed to do jobs about the house when he did not have work outside. 'They let me stay there for three years until I got a place in the army.' From the age of thirty-seven to forty-three, corresponding to the six years of the war, he spent the whole time as an army private stationed in England. He liked the life, and was discharged with a good character. He then went to lodge with his brother and sister-in-law and worked as a railway porter. His sister-in-law looked after him in a kindly way, but he just sat in the house idly staring at the fire, getting in everyone's way, and scrounging small sums from the children. He became such an embarrassment when the daughters of the house came of an age to want to bring their boy friends home, that finally his sister-in-law pretended she had had a note from the housing authority to say that she must not keep a lodger. Even then it was months before she was able to edge him out. He declined her offer to find him a furnished room, and reverted to former habits of irregular work, stopping at hostels, breaking in, and getting caught at once. When he was aged 50, he had his first period on probation. According to the Probation Officer's report he attended regularly but 'sat like a sack'. He was apathetic and unwilling to stick to any job for long, though several were found for him.

The example just quoted clearly belonged to the group of inadequate personality deviants. The man's outstanding peculiarities were deadly apathy, lack of initiative, and social isolation. His relatives remarked that he had never been known to have a friend of either sex. At interview he gave an impression of dullness, both intellectual and emotional. On formal testing, his intelligence was found to be a dull normal, with an I.Q. of 86 on the full-scale *Wechsler*. His answers in the test were blurred and frequently off the point and he was very slow and weak in common sense. He seemed mildly but chronically depressed. During the interviews he had to be prompted continually, producing nothing spontaneously. On being pressed for personal particulars he was apt to become tearful and semi-inarticulate. None of this amounted to a definite illness, but he would certainly be described in psychiatric terms as a dull, inadequate personality. Had he presented himself at an out-patient clinic he would probably have been given anti-depressive drugs if not electro-convulsive therapy.

A reasonable argument could be made for regarding such a man as an example of the 'affectionless' character described by Bowlby, one whose personality development has been arrested as a result of emotional deprivation in childhood. He appeared to have nursed a grievance against his mother for he said at interview that she never visited them while they were away in a residential school, although his brother said she did. The brother, who was interviewed, had many characteristics in common with the prisoner. He had no criminal record, but he was of dishevelled appearance and dull and lifeless in expression. The brother's wife explained that he was a liability as a husband, often out of work, stubborn and difficult in temperament, emotionally dependent upon her and financially dependent upon his children. He suffered from asthma and insomnia. She said she had always had 'to treat him like a child'.

In this instance there was no difficulty about including the prisoner among the group classed as having had a genuinely crime-free period. The man himself, although he was ready to admit culpability at other times, maintained that he had been honest during the period in question. All the social evidence, including his army record and the detailed evidence of his sister-in-law, tended to support the prisoner's claim.

In some cases the genuineness or otherwise of the crime-free period was less easily decided. On the whole those prisoners who were least truthful and most evasive at interview were the ones least likely to have had a genuine gap. Of the six who either refused to allow a home visit or else gave a false address (49), four were thought never to have had any genuine gap.

Case 5

A married man, aged thirty-seven. He had two findings of guilt as a juvenile and ten convictions as an adult, all for offences against property, including larceny, housebreaking, forgery and false pretences. He had spent periods in approved school and Borstal. His criminal record showed a gap of six years at liberty between his seventh and eighth adult convictions.

The prisoner denied having committed any serious offence during this time, but admitted that at no time was he 'scrupulously honest'. While working in grocers' shops during the period of the gap, he sold goods at incorrect prices and pocketed the difference, but he said that was common practice and hardly criminal. Later, while working in a railway booking office, he obliged people with illegal travel vouchers. He continued this practice after leaving the railway, using a pad of stolen blank vouchers. He was caught and convicted after he had been doing this for about five years. His wife maintained that he had never really interrupted his dishonest activities and that during the greater part of the conviction-free period he was swindling the railway. Before that he had made some effort to remain honest. At a moment when he was expressing great remorse following a conviction for stealing zinc, she got him to agree to give her his wage packet intact and let her manage their finances, but he soon defaulted from this arrangement, lost his job, and reverted to his customary habits.

In personality he was, according to his wife, 'full of charm' and 'liked by everybody'. He loved to talk to anybody prepared to listen to his stories, which mostly consisted of elaborate embroideries designed to put himself in a favourable light. She believed he thought himself perfect, with no ability for self-criticism whatsoever. He was very lively and restless, always plotting hare-brained schemes for making money quickly. She said she could 'almost hear his brain ticking'. Since his marriage, he had had a great variety of employments, most of them 'rather high flown'. He talks his way in everywhere, but never stays long. His latest employment was peddling vacuum cleaners with a partner. They registered as a firm and called themselves directors, but had no cash. She said it was a pleasant change to have the security of National Assistance while her husband was in prison.

The wife's version of his characteristics was amply confirmed by the prisoner's behaviour at interview, at which he was most fluent and plausible, and produced detailed explanations of some of his offences, which subsequent enquiry showed to be quite false. He was above average in intelligence (I.Q. 113 on the full-scale *Wechsler*) and able to make his stories convincing. He mentioned that his mother was a lady almoner at a particular hospital. Enquiry showed that her only connection with hospitals was occasional employment as a cook. He mentioned that he ran a youth club for three years until he had to relinquish it on being convicted for defrauding the railway. Actually, he did youth club work for a few months only. He started off with a flourish but soon quarrelled with the committee and was asked to leave.

The prisoner had definite aggressive traits. He was one of the very few in the series who had been disciplined during their present sentence for fighting. He had also been dismissed from his employment with the railways following an incident in which he struck a passenger. His wife also mentioned that he had 'furious tempers' and that he would sometimes 'lash out' at her if she tried to dissuade him from something he wanted to do.

In spite of all these shortcomings, the prisoner was an affectionate family man and devoted to his two young children. His wife, who had been married to him for fifteen years, was sure she would never want to leave him, even though she knew he was unfaithful to her. At interview the prisoner remarked, without prompting: 'I've got strong ideas about sex. It should be confined to the bedroom and between married people. I've never wanted to go outside. I don't like the idea of nude shows. I detest homosexuals in any shape or form.'

The prisoner and his wife gave independent and somewhat contrasting accounts of his upbringing. His wife felt that he had never enjoyed normal affection from either parent. His father was a bombastic, self-opinionated man who brought up his children strictly and without much show of affection. The father was estranged from his own mother, and although the old lady lived next door, he never spoke a word to her till the day she died. The prisoner gave a more idealised picture, and said his mother was an affectionate character, who tried to keep peace between her children and her husband. He admitted, however, that she was extremely bitter towards him since his convictions, and had written him a letter saying he had given her years of misery and she wanted no more to do with him. She had not answered his wife's letters and she had taken no interest in her grandchildren.

The prisoner had two elder brothers and a younger sister, all married. The sister was very houseproud and unfriendly, on bad terms with her mother, and strikingly unaffectionate towards her only son. One brother was described by the prisoner as 'strong-willed' and not one to stand for any 'back-chat', and unhappily married to a much older woman. The prisoner also alleged that this brother used to thieve but had escaped detection. He described his older brother as 'a bullying type like father, with a stutter and an inferiority complex. His wife has left him several times'.

The above example shows a man who was erratic and unreliable in his occupations, boastful and insincere in his personal relations, and at times impulsively and rashly aggressive or inconsiderate to his remarkably tolerant wife and family. He was therefore classed as a personality deviant, although not one of the more extreme cases. He was clearly one of the active-aggressive type of deviant from a typically rejectant home. His crimes were actively motivated, he liked to plan and scheme and was pleased with himself if he succeeded. He was more resourceful than any inadequate and quite capable of handling a job of work, even while exploiting it for purposes of fraud. It was clear that this man had no genuinely crime-free gap. Indeed, with such a self-satisfied character, whose crimes were a means of self assertion and not at all dictated by necessity, it is difficult to envisage him ever having a long period free from crime.

Summing up, it appears that out of a total of fifty-nine men (including nine preventive detainees) who showed an apparent 'gap' in their records, only sixty per cent (i.e. thirty-five men) were considered to have had a genuinely crime-free interlude. These thirty-five men had had a total of forty-one 'genuine' gaps. No man had had more than two. The genuine gaps ranged in duration from four and a half to seventeen years, with an average of seven years seven months.[1] The thirty-three gaps classed as 'false' averaged almost as long, namely six years nine months, so mere length of time was no guarantee of genuineness.

2. Gaps in Relation to Types of Deviance

The two examples just quoted draw attention to the connection between personality type and likelihood of having a crime-free gap. Table 17 shows how the prisoners with genuine gaps were distributed among the personality groupings. The inadequates had far the largest proportion of genuine cases. This finding is unlikely to have been due to bias in the investigator. In most cases the evidence for deciding whether to class the gaps as genuine or false came from the social enquiries and the examination of Scotland Yard records, and these investigations took place after the psychiatric classifications were completed.

The impression produced by these figures, and amply confirmed by examination of individual histories, was that the inadequates

[1] This does not necessarily reflect the true length of time free from offences, since gaps were classed as genuine so long as they had a minimum of four years crime-free. Offences known to have occurred towards the end of a long gap would not cause the whole to be rejected as false.

revealed themselves as feeble and hesitant in the pursuit of their criminal careers as in other matters. The more determined and resolute individuals, those especially who approached closest to normal personalities, once having embarked upon criminal ways, tended to continue more consistently and relentlessly, and to have less compunction about identifying themselves as unrepentant and unremitting thieves. The following example is a case in point:

Case 9

A married man of fifty-two, convicted on nine occasions, all for offences against property. He admitted cheerfully that, since he started thieving at the age of twenty-five, he had never stopped for any length of time. He had one apparent gap in his record, lasting nearly five years, which coincided in part with a period of wartime service in the army.

He was a cheerful, candid, unworried informant, of plump, rubicund appearance and equable manner. Reared in a respectable, united, working-class family, with no noticeable deprivations or lack of affection, he had one younger brother who was a normally honest family-man and steady worker. Mother, he said, was boss in the house, but she was doting and indulgent with her sons. The prisoner progressed normally at school, mixed easily, liked sports and was, he said, 'nearly always made monitor and never got the stick'.

He had always been a friendly, easy-going individual and not shy of girls. He married at twenty-five, and his wife confirmed that he had been an affectionate husband who always came back to her in spite of his irregular way of life. They had three daughters, who grew up healthily and all made satisfactory marriages, and two sons, still at school and doing well. At the home visit, their house was noted to be shabby and devoid of luxuries, with the exception of a television set and two well-cared-for pets.

On leaving school the prisoner worked for six years as a butcher's assistant, but finally left because he could not get increased wages. After that he never settled to a steady job, and his wife confirmed that during the whole of their married life he just 'picked up jobs on race-tracks'. The prisoner said that he was first introduced to thieving and housebreaking and disposing of goods via market-stalls by a friendly family living next door, all of whom were professional criminals.

When called up for the army at the commencement of the war, when he was thirty-one, he liked it at first, but after some nasty experiences at Dunkirk he decided he would not go abroad again, and thereafter he repeatedly went absent or deserted. He was finally embarked for the Near East while still under detention. He says he settled down well for the two years he was away as he had no option, although records showed that he went sick with complaints of recurrent backache diagnosed as fibrositis.

The prisoner's only outstanding characteristics were summed up by his wife. She reported that he hated regular hours, frequently got up late and was an inveterate gambler. She felt that he liked money too much and would do anything to get it. Even at times when he could afford it, however, he never gave her a regular allowance and never treated his family to holidays or outings. Nevertheless, he was an affectionate man and all the family were fond of him and tolerant of his behaviour. The neighbours had a good word for him. Although his peculiarities were obvious, they were not extreme enough for him to be classed as a personality deviant.

Although the figures were too small to furnish an adequate control, a similar trend appeared when the preventive detainees were considered from the point of view of conviction-free intervals. Applying exactly the same criteria to them, gaps were found in the records of nine out of the fifty men and were classed as genuine in five cases, four of whom were inadequates. Summing up the observation so far, they suggest that genuine interludes of honesty in the careers of persistent thieves, though always exceptional, are somewhat commoner among offenders of passive-inadequate type. This conclusion was strengthened by an analysis of the background circumstances of the genuine gaps the results of which supplied some plausible explanations for the connection between gaps and inadequacy.

3. Circumstances Associated with Genuine Gaps

In a few instances the genuine gaps corresponded with some obvious special circumstances. Thus, in two cases (29, 87), both psychotics, with three gaps between them, each episode corresponded almost exactly with periods spent as patients in mental hospitals, relapse following almost immediately they were discharged. In eleven cases, the period of a genuine gap, or at least a substantial part of it, coincided with a period of service in the armed forces. Among these eleven men, the lapse back into crime occurred in six cases within a year of discharge. Service records showed that only one of them (38) relapsed while still in the forces. These eleven cases, in which military service appeared to be an important factor, were predominantly inadequates, including only two aggressives and one non-deviant. On the whole, the aggressive tended to resent military discipline and to rebel. In contrast, the well ordered and relatively simplified routine of military service made a favourable impact on some inadequates, as seen in the following example:

Case 4

This was a single man, aged thirty-eight, with seventeen convictions and eleven sentences of imprisonment, all for stealing. He confessed to thieving from home since the age of fourteen, and he was first charged at the age of seventeen, by his father. After that, apart from the gap under investigation, only one full year of his life was spent at liberty and free of convictions. The gap consisted of a period of eight years, seven and a half of which were spent in the army, in which he served as a cook.

His mother died soon after he was born, and he was at first reared by over-indulgent grandparents. At an early age he was taken over by his father and a new step-mother. The latter provided for him well materially, but disapproved his attachment to his grandparents. He felt that she was always complaining and nagging and favouring her own children. She and his father were both sternly respectable and horrified by his dishonesty and lying.

He was a timid, shy child who was bullied because he was afraid to fight. He wet the bed till he was twelve. He led an isolated unsettled life without friends. He obtained employments easily, usually as a cook, but rarely kept his jobs long. He would feel moody and fed-up and then either run off with some money from work or go out and steal a bicycle. He gave himself up voluntarily to the police many times. He admitted that although he disliked prison he felt somehow 'less insecure' inside. He liked the company of men, especially homosexuals. His sexual fantasies were homosexual although, he said, he had never indulged overtly. His happiest period was in the army. He 'fiddled' rations the same as the others, but never felt the impulse to steal money and was discharged with a 'fair' character. He was punished on twelve occasions for breaches of military discipline, such as short periods of absence and neglect of equipment, but he was said to be a good worker. He admitted resuming his thieving habits immediately he was discharged from the army.

On release from prison after being interviewed for this research he attended a psychiatric out-patient clinic. The consultant's summing up was: 'An extremely insecure, dependent man who needs to form a safe dependent relationship in order to keep out of trouble.'

The commonest circumstances associated with genuine gaps, commoner still than military service, was the establishment of some stable human relationship, usually of a dependent or semi-parasitic quality, but nevertheless effective in bringing about a cessation of crime for at least as long as the relationship lasted. One good example of this has already been quoted (Case 1, page 35) in which the prisoner remained honest until his sister-in-law, who had been supporting and mothering him, decided she could no longer have him around the house. Another instance of the same kind was the following:

Case 6

This was a single man of forty-four. At interview he gave an impression of mental subnormality, but on testing his I.Q. was 86 on the full-scale *Wechsler*, a result within the dull normal range. He had a severe left-sided hemiplegic paralysis and deformity, said to have followed head injuries in a road accident at the age of twenty-one.

He was first convicted of stealing at the age of fifteen, and was convicted on a total of twenty-two occasions for similar offences. He mostly stole bicycles or took cash from gas-meters. From the age of thirty-five to thirty-nine he had a conviction-free period of four years nine months, after which he was convicted for stealing bicycles and was put on probation for two years. He had a further period of four years four months free, until his latest conviction and imprisonment, which was once again for stealing bicycles.

He was the only child of a late marriage, both his parents having been previously widowed. His father was over sixty when he was born and died during his adolescence. Soon after this he was sent to an approved school. He settled there happily enough once he was removed sufficient distance to make absconding home to mother difficult. He became a 'boxing champion' at the school. His serious injury and resulting disability was the consequence of taking a relative's car without permission and crashing it at high speed. He never adjusted himself to his changed circumstances. He ran away from a training school for cripples. He constantly complained of the impossibility of finding work and relied largely on national assistance. He led an isolated life on account of his shyness and over-sensitivity about his deformity. He was described by his probation officer as a spineless, work-shy man who was virtually unable to do anything for himself and was very dependent upon his mother during her lifetime. He lived with his mother, who was doting and over-indulgent, until the age of thirty-five. She then had to go into hospital, having been ailing many years, and finally died in a mental hospital. He was married for a short time at the age of thirty-one to a foreign girl, but they soon broke up. He said she was hasty-tempered and nagged him and did not get on with his mother, with whom they were both living.

The gap in his record of convictions, which was from the age of thirty-five to thirty-nine, corresponded with the efforts of a motherly widow, an ex-nurse and old friend of his mother, who took him into her home when his mother died. Besides being protective, she was also firmer than his mother, and insisted that he kept regular hours and tried to obtain work. He was lovable and affectionate in return, and looked after her when she was ill. Sometimes, however, his frustrations would get the better of him and he would storm about the house in a temper, and then break down in tears. His first lapse, while lodging with this widow, occurred at a time when she was hard pressed for money and food and he was having genuine difficulty in obtaining either a job or assistance money. He pretended to her that he had found a job with a cycle repairer, but the bicycles were stolen.

After being caught and placed on probation for two years, he resumed his good behaviour and started work as a cinema attendant. Four years later, the widow announced that she could not give him shelter much longer as she intended to re-marry. He then visited the probation officer asking for help, but was referred to the National Assistance Board. He thereupon relapsed again into bicycle stealing, and when convicted for his latest offences there were three charges and forty-two similar cases taken into consideration.

The widow who befriended him was interviewed. She was a proudly respectable old lady who gave an impression of truthfulness. She was aware of the prisoner's lapses, and of the circumstances which occasioned them, and she could confirm his periods of apparent honesty. She was very sorry for the prisoner, whom she looked upon as an erring son, but was firm that she was not in a position to take him back to live in her house. The local police confirmed that the prisoner spoke 'the approximate truth' about his offences, and the widow was 'as honest as the day'.

In at least eighteen cases, as in the above example, a genuine gap could be plausibly attributed to some kind of protective relationship, the lapse back into crime occurring when, for some reason usually beyond the prisoner's control, the relationship came to an end. Thus, eight men relapsed following the death or defection of a wife or cohabitee. In fact, marriage or cohabitation played an important part in many genuine gaps, especially in the cases of those prisoners who allowed their women to assume a motherly, protective role. In some cases (e.g. 13, 27, 38, 46) prisoners responded in this way to older women of more dominant character although associations with other younger women had had no effect upon their criminal habits. Once again, it was the inadequates who most often found themselves these sheltered relationships and were able to profit from them. Thirteen out of eighteen such cases were from the inadequate group. The following examples provide brief illustrations of some variations on this common theme displayed by individual inadequates:

Case 13

A single man of forty-nine, an excessive drinker, and generally feckless and irresponsible. In spite of a superficial gay bravado, he was a fundamentally insecure person who worried a lot about his thieving. On occasions he had been driven by fear into surrendering to the police. He was the only son of a strict and dominating mother. He was shy with women and with the exception of a period as a conscript, during which he got into trouble through drinking, he lived with his mother until the late thirties.

He had two gaps. The first, which lasted four years six months, was while living with and being looked after by his widowed mother after his discharge from the army. When she decided to go to live with her married daughter, and he was left to fend for himself, he lasted only a couple of months before being arrested. His second gap, lasting nine years, coincided exactly with an association with a married woman of mature years. She was his landlady, and bored with her own husband. She liked a 'good time' and went out to work with the prisoner selling ices and both making and spending money heavily. Eventually she left her husband and set up with the prisoner a small business. The strain was too much for him, he lost interest and left her. Within three months he was again in prison.

Case 20

A physically puny, weak natured and chronically neurotic drug addict. As a child he had lost both parents from pulmonary tuberculosis and had himself been ill with the disease. He had one long crime-free gap of ten years coinciding with his marriage to a hospital nurse, whom he had met as a patient. His relapse occurred when his wife, being pregnant, went back to her parents on account of his heavy drinking and demands that she have an abortion because he did not want children. He responded to her departure with a suicidal attempt, followed soon after by offences connected with drug-taking.

Case 27

A divorced man, aged thirty-five. He first married at nineteen, but his wife left him on account of his heavy drinking and general irresponsibility. He then lived with a succession of women, including a prostitute, associated with criminals and thieving persistently all the while. He was a moody character who once attempted suicide. He habitually squandered his gains in lavishness towards acquaintances met casually in public houses.

He had one genuine gap lasting six years, which corresponded exactly with a period of cohabitation with a woman ten years older. She controlled his money and went to work to help to support him. His relapse occurred when she left him because she had an offer of marriage from another man.

Case 35

A single man of fifty-eight with a history of numerous offences of larceny. Subsequently to being seen for this research he was sentenced to preventive detention. In spite of considerable ability in well-paid administrative posts, he was a friendless, secretive character and a solitary drinker. He was sexually impotent and had perverse inclinations, and he spent a lot of time brooding over his misfortunes in this respect.

He had two gaps, the first one entirely spurious, due to a period of imprisonment abroad not being recorded on his file. He had one genuine gap, lasting eleven years, during which he was in a residential job working for an elderly woman employer whom he liked. He relapsed almost at once when she retired and sold the business.

Case 38

A widower aged fifty-nine, reared in a respectable, middle-class home and given a public-school education, he had repeated convictions for stealing and for forging accounts. He was a rash borrower and spendthrift, and was said to have drunk his way through a substantial inheritance. He had two genuine gaps. The first, as a young man, was unexplained, and ended with a court martial for falsifying army accounts. At the age of forty-seven he married for the first time a widow older still than himself. His second gap lasted for six years from the beginning of their association till her death.

Case 50

A morose, unmarried social isolate aged thirty. He had been rejected by his mother and reared in an orphanage. A friend said he was shy, especially with women, although he tried to counteract it with bombastic behaviour. He had one gap of six years while he was lodging with a sympathetic landlord who took an interest in him. At the same time he had a religious conversion and devoted himself to street corner evangelism. On leaving his friendly lodging and going to stay in a hostel he quickly lapsed back into crime.

Apart from relapses following the break-up of some established relationship, there were few examples of gaps coming to an end through unusually severe stress. In one instance (22) a relapse occurred in the face of financial troubles due to the failure of a business into which the prisoner and his wife had put a lot of effort. His criminal brother's arrival from Eire at the same time provided the last straw. But such a cocantation of woes was unusual. This particular prisoner was not a personality deviant. In the case of the inadequates, once their protective umbrella dissolved, stresses no greater than everyday demands proved amply sufficient to provoke relapse.

The bulk of the genuine gaps occurred in the inadequate prisoners at times when they were in sheltered circumstances. There remained a puzzling minority which corresponded to no identifiable social factors and were not necessarily associated with inadequacy. These included some instances of dubious authenticity, which were classed with the genuine gaps because they fulfilled the formal criteria, but which carried little conviction and generally lack confirmation. The following is a typical example:

Case 33

An aggressive work-shy man of thirty-seven. He married at twenty-one, but made no effort to support his wife and continued habits of sexual promiscuity. He was of very dull intelligence (I.Q. 72), had had hospital treatment for outbursts of temper, and been discharged from the forces with a diagnosis of 'hysterical psychopathy'. He had one gap of eight years. The first part of this coincided with a period of cohabitation with a woman who worked to support him. When she became pregnant her parents, with whom they were living, turned him out. His situation during the remainder of the gap could not be discovered.

The active-aggressive type of personality deviant, and also the non-deviants, when they did have genuine gaps — which was less often than the inadequates — seemed more in control of their situation, less dependent upon immediate circumstances. Whereas the inadequates relapsed in a passive way, following someone else's action in withdrawing support, the others were more often the instigators of their own downfall. Thus, in an example quoted in a previous section (Case 7, page 28), an aggressive deviant gave up a superior job because he thought the life of a street-trader more appealing. The connection between gaps and marital or social situation, although present in all types of case, was closer and more essential in the inadequate than in the others. For example, two aggressive deviants (8, 24), each with a gap coincident with courtship and marriage, relapsed without any change in their domestic situations, but as a result of loss of temper and assault leading to loss of job and return to thieving:

Case 8

A man of twenty-nine, married to a woman of twenty-two, and father of a child of three. He was first convicted at the age of eleven for breaking in, and subsequently was convicted on five occasions as an adult. Two of these convictions were for causing actual bodily harm. His latest offence was committed with another man. They waited for a laundry employee who carried cash for the staff wages, snatched her bag containing the money, and made off in a stolen car.

He was a healthy, tough-looking man. He refused to allow his wife to be visited because, he said, she had already been upset by one visitor from the prison. He was reasonably friendly at interview, although somewhat aggressive in manner. He had been involved in a fight with another prisoner, which he explained by saying, 'A red-band tried to order me around so I hit him.' He was excitably anti-authoritarian in attitude. He described the prison visiting booths as 'those animal boxes — worse than the cat! I've seen men come out of them raving.' He said he could not stand jobs where the foreman throws his weight about. 'I can't stand being ordered around.'

His parents were respectable and hard-working. His father died when he was fifteen and he had a step-father. He said his mother was 'always knocking us children about — lovey-dovey one moment and clouting you the next. Everything had to be her way.' He had one elder brother, also married and also a prisoner. As a child of eight or nine he was separated from his parents due to wartime evacuation, but was brought back home again 'when father found me covered in bruises'. At school he liked sports and boxing and had lots of friends, but he felt the teachers 'didn't seem to care about us and made us work carrying milk bottles and things'.

According to the probation report, he mixed with a tough, delinquent crowd of youths. After trying several jobs, he joined the navy at eighteen, liked it and served satisfactorily for a year until he was discharged on account of an ear infection. At twenty he was reconvicted and put on probation. While still on probation he was reconvicted for assault. He said: 'I had a fight with a man who tried to push us out of a café. There was no need to come round bustling and poking us. He got what he asked for.' He was given a further period of probation and after that things went smoothly. The probation officer noted that under the good influence of his fiancée he gave up his former rowdy associates and saved to get married. This was the period of his 'gap' which lasted five years until he was reconvicted as a result of 'celebrating' with some workmates on Christmas Eve and becoming involved in a brawl in a café. 'The police picked on me just because I had a record' he said. After this he was unemployed and began to steal again. The police called at his house to question him, so he 'went on the run'. 'I thought then that as they treated us like criminals I might as well be one.' He and a friend thereupon planned the wages snatch which led to his latest imprisonment.

Summing up the conclusions of this section, it seems that substantial conviction-free periods in established criminal careers are unusual and that when they do occur at least two-fifths can be shown to be due to successful evasion of arrest rather than to genuine interruption of criminal activity. The classification of prisoners into passive-inadequates and active-aggressives, which was previously shown to distinguish some broad trends in criminal behaviour, also proved helpful in the understanding of the background of the genuine crime-free interludes. Such interludes were commonest in the inadequate group and tended to coincide with sheltered circumstances, such as residence in an institution, periods of military service, or, most frequent and most important, the establishment of a relationship with some stronger personality, someone able and willing to provide continuous sympathy and practical support and in effect to assume the role of mother substitute. The aggressives were mostly too self-assertive and independent to submit to motherly guidance by wives or control by military authorities. Such crime-free periods as they had, which were few, started and stopped on their own initiative, whereas the inadequates tended to change with fluctuations in their domestic circumstances.

Even among inadequates only a minority have crime-free interludes. Many are so solitary and peculiar that they cannot form relationships with the people who might help them, and even the limited demands made upon them in the services prove too much. Nevertheless, the finding that at least some inadequates will respond to mothering suggests possible measures of after-care. It may have to be recognised that there exists a class of hopelessly damaged personalities who require permanent supervision and support if they are not to spend the larger part of their lives in prison. One useful function of psychiatric classification is to distinguish such inadequates from other offenders for whom the spoon-feeding approach would be futile, if not an aggravating insult.

VI

ILLNESSES

1. Physical Ailments

THE most frequent and important deviations from the norm lay in the field of personality, in the large number of difficult and peculiar characters. In addition some prisoners also displayed symptoms of definite illness, occasionally physical, much more often mental. In physique and appearance the men were frequently described as 'average', and most of them had been fit and strong for most of their lives, although a few were beginning for the first time to experience the infirmities natural to old age. Nevertheless, although only a minority were physically afflicted, the incidence of physical illness and handicap was higher than might be expected among a population of working men of similar age. For instance, out of the hundred prisoners,[1] one had died of cancer of the stomach, and another had been under treatment for cancer of the throat. Three had had peptic ulcers and a fourth was still acutely ill with this condition and had to be interviewed in his hospital bed (88). Five others were semi-invalids, two more were severe cripples and several had minor disabilities or a history of recurrent illness.[2]

Indications of possible brain damage were found in a few cases only. One man (51) had had severe epilepsy when young and another (34) was still having to take anti-convulsants for controlling his fits. Five men had had severe head injuries in childhood or youth, in one case (6) resulting in permanent paralysis.

The fact that many of the prisoners had drifted for years with no settled home outside of institutions or common lodging houses may have taken some toll. Although no objective criteria were used, the interviews left the impression that an undue proportion of the men were prematurely ageing.

[1] These do not include the two excluded from the series for medical reasons, one preventive detainee of advanced age who died from coronary thrombosis, and one intermittent recidivist under treatment for peptic ulcer and too ill to be interviewed.

[2] Diagnoses were made as follows: 2 cancer (69, 60 — deceased); 2 epilepsy (34 51 — recovered); 2 cripples (6 — traumatic hemiplegia, 41 — poliomyelitis); 5 semi-invalids (20 — lung abscess, 65 — diabetes, 87 — angina pectoris, 59 — emphysema, 90 — hyperpiesis); 5 serious head injuries (6, 26, 36, 88, 92).

2. Psychosis

No matter what criteria were used, these habitual prisoners, and particularly the preventive detainees, showed an extraordinarily high incidence of psychiatric morbidity. Ten cases (8 P.D.'s) were or had been psychotic. Six of these were or had been certified insane. A further nine (5 P.D.'s) had at some time been admitted to hospital for treatment of psychiatric disorder. A further seven (4 P.D.'s), in addition to five of those mentioned above, had been recommended for discharge from the armed forces on psychiatric grounds. Many showed pronounced neurotic symptons and some had deep-rooted sexual perversions.

Naturally there was some overlap, since some prisoners displayed several pathological signs simultaneously. Ignoring the manifestations of personality deviation and the various degrees of social maladaptation, and counting only those symptons which all psychiatrists would agree indicate serious mental pathology, then at a conservative estimate at least a third of the prisoners were suffering from, or had not fully recovered from, mental illnesses of considerable severity. Put another way, if these men had not been criminals or personality deviants, and had presented themselves with these symptons at a psychiatric clinic, then at least a third would have been taken on as patients and of these a half might have been thought ill enough to be admitted to hospital.

The incidence of real insanity was surprisingly high, especially among the preventive detainees, seven of whom were actively psychotic. Only one of the fifty intermittent recidivists (29) appeared psychotic at interview. This was a widower aged eighty who had been repeatedly hospitalised for attacks of manic-depressive psychosis. He was excitably garrulous and expressed grandiose delusions of wealth and property. In addition to these eight active psychotics, another two men (36, 79) had been previously certified insane.

Their high incidence of psychosis during imprisonment does not prove that preventive detainees are more abnormal than other recidivists. The fact that they remain so long in detention means that their breakdowns inevitably occur in prison. Among recidivists who shuttle in and out quickly, the incipient psychotic has less time to develop an obtrusive illness while in prison. He also stands a greater chance of avoiding imprisonment subsequently, either by revealing obvious madness at one of his numerous appearances in court, or by admission to mental hospital during one of his spells at liberty.

The commonest form of psychosis among the prisoners was paranoid schizophrenia which manifested in florid form (i.e. delusions, hallucinations, confusion of thought, and inappropriate or blunted emotion) in five preventive detainees. Two of these (51, 83) had been certified and transferred to outside mental hospitals, the other three (87, 91, 95) were under care in prison hospitals. There was no dispute as to diagnosis in any of these cases. Here is one example, others are given in Appendix I.

Case 95

Aged fifty-eight when sentenced to preventive detention, this man was interviewed three years later. He looked ageing and decrepit. He was careless of his appearance and completely preoccupied with a system of persecutory delusions about a conspiracy to keep him in prison. He arrived with an untidy bundle of documents intended to explain his 'case' against the authorities. The extent of his thought disorder was well shown in his letters, of which the following is an example:

> 'Silence at this particular moment: Why? I have to refrain in making any further comments: which may be accepting the essence of diplomacy to remain dormant under "DURESS" subject to The Secrecy Act and supported by the misuse of the Crown Prerogative by means in claiming Crown Privilege. Being the object in view to pervert the true course of justice being established contrary to the Documentary Evidence Act. The interpretation in Law, CORRUPTION, KNOWINGLY! The above kind of Conspiracy and Corruption has been in operation for years. KNOWINGLY on behalf of Whitehall and further supported by legal Professional Chicanery.
>
> 'State Dictatorship by means of "MAKE BELIEF" has had its days based on State BLUFF!
>
> 'I am now fully in possession of the Master Trump-Card. The longer of a delayed action declared by myself: The Greater the Damages subject to Evasion, Frustration and Abstraction: That will now prove in itself all in my favour to justify Gross Damages.'

Although his mental condition had slowly deteriorated during the present detention, his persecutory delusions had been present for some years before and were noted by the psychologist during the allocation centre examinations. The man had served one previous sentence of preventive detention. In their report to the Court, the prison commissioners found nothing in his physical or mental condition to suggest that he was unsuitable for a further period of preventive detention.

In addition to the five just mentioned, a further two preventive detainees were considered psychotic at the time they were interviewed although their condition was not officially recorded by the prison medical authorities. One had paranoid delusions (84), another was confused and irrational but free from coherently expressed delusions (68). Both are described in Appendix I. In addition, one of the intermittent recidivists (36), who had spent many years in mental hospitals as a certified patient, was considered to be on the borderline of psychosis at the time he was seen. During one of his hospital admissions he had almost murdered another patient for no apparent reason (see page 74). The only instance of actual psychosis among the intermittent recidivists (29) was in an excitable condition bordering on mania, and was voicing grandiose but unfounded ideas about his possessions and connections (see page 54).

None of the hundred prisoners showed symptoms of very severe depression, accompanied by melancholic delusions or active suicidal tendencies, such that they could have been considered psychotic. However, about six were quite badly depressed, enough to have been taken on for active treatment had they presented themselves at a psychiatric clinic. One of the preventive detainees (79) had had psychotic depressions in the past and did not appear to be fully recovered. His history was of special interest because, unlike any of the paranoid cases, the fluctuations of his mental state did appear to be closely associated with the commission of offences:

Case 79

A divorced man of thirty eight who had ten convictions for thieving offences and one for 'sleeping out'. He had been out of touch with his wife and other relatives for many years, and refused to allow them to be visited, because, he said, he was too ashamed. He was of no fixed abode and his offences were all committed alone. He was in the habit of wandering aimlessly about the country, breaking into houses to obtain food and cash. On the last occasion he had been out of prison only three weeks before he gave himself up to the police. Asked why he had done so he said 'I had to face the inevitable sooner or later. It's got to be one charge or a hundred. I expected to get P.D.' On various occasions during previous wanderings he had presented himself at police stations or hospitals saying he could not remember who he was.

Although his mother died when he was about five, he had an apparently normal upbringing by devoted grandparents, and was in no sort of trouble until aged twenty. He then met and married a dull and probably unsatisfactory wife. He complained that she was unfaithful to him. At this point his previously satisfactory behaviour in the navy changed, he over-stayed his leaves and took to heavy drinking. He was finally discharged on psychiatric grounds with 'reactive depression' associated with his domestic situation.

His wife complained to his doctors that after his discharge from the navy he never worked, except for a week or two here and there, and that he kept wandering away from home and spending all his money on drink. Once when arrested at age twenty-five, and twice when serving sentences of imprisonment, at ages twenty-five and twenty-seven, he was certified insane and placed in mental hospitals. On the last occasion, the medical notes recorded: 'foolish and irresponsible and becomes restless at times'. 'He is hallucinated and hears a voice which tells him to move from place to place to his ultimate end. The voice has told him to kill himself.' At interview he rationalised all these episodes as sheer malingering, but the prison medical officers were sure that this was not a feasible explanation. He admitted that his periods of wandering were compulsive, and accompanied by feelings of dejection and helplessness. He expressed much self-blame and guilt. 'I know I could have done better. I don't blame anybody but myself. It makes you feel pretty small telling all this sort of thing. . . .' There seemed little doubt that he was a man of depressive temperament, and subject to periodic psychotic or near psychotic breakdowns.

Of the five other prisoners suffering from lesser degrees of psychiatric depression, the following is a typical example:

Case 89

This was a man aged sixty-seven, who had been under treatment for cancer of the throat. He repeatedly expressed feelings of worthlessness and hopelessness and said he hoped he would die in prison as there seemed no prospects for him outside. He remarked that when he was admitted to hospital for treatment he had felt he wouldn't mind if he died. He reproached himself for the 'real wrong' he had done in his life of crime. He complained that he was easily upset by trivial incidents, which would provoke spells of trembling and crying. Although he had been a cook, he would not occupy himself in prison cooking because, he said, he found it too depressing. He was somewhat slow and confused in his talk, but it was difficult to decide whether this was due to his emotional state or to senile changes. He had been under supervision in the prison hospital, but there was no note of poor sleeping or eating, and he was not regarded by the prison medical officer as a depressed patient, although he was recorded as irritable and showing signs of senility.

3. Neurosis

Manifest psychiatric disturbance was by no means limited to the ten latent or active psychotics. A further forty-three men (including twenty-four of the P.D.'s) complained of symptoms of neurotic type. These took the form of headaches or physical complaints with no organic basis, hypochondriacal fears, specific phobias, feelings of tension, irrational anxiety, unexplained depression, or preoccupation with ideas of inferiority. Had the prisoners consisted of a series of patients referred for psychiatric examination they could hardly have shown a greater incidence of mental symptoms. In few cases, however, were the symptoms so acute or so severe that they would have compelled a working man of ordinary personality to take sick leave.

Some prisoners appeared to dramatise or to exaggerate their symptoms, but the majority of those who brought forward complaints did in fact show signs of a generally anxious, worrying disposition, or of unhappy, unsettled attitudes, indicative of the presence of genuine mental conflict. They differed from typical neurotics at out-patient clinics in that their symptoms were diffuse and of great chronicity and produced in response to a wide range of stresses. There were none whose symptoms were confined to special situations. Although many of them were apt to commit offences at times of difficulty or frustration, there were none whose offences took the form of a compulsive neurotic ritual. Like the psychotic breakdowns, these neurotic disturbances manifested as an additional complication in immature or deviant personalities, and did not account for the full extent of their disorder. Far from saving them from mental conflict or neurosis, which personality deviation is sometimes said to do, their underlying lack of ego resources seemed to render them, if anything, all the more prone to symptoms. The inadequate group, especially, contained a high proportion with manifest neurotic complaints.

The following is a typical example of the neurotic disturbance displayed by many of these prisoners:

Case 96

This was a married man aged forty-six, separated from his wife, but living in hopes that she would take him back, although by all accounts their married life had been one long squabble. At interview he complained of depression, and was in fact several times on the verge of tears. He also said he was off his food, sleeping badly, and concerned about nervous jerkings which he experienced at the moment of falling asleep.

At the age of eighteen he was described in a Borstal report as 'very miserable and depressed; makes a very poor impression as far as physique and character are concerned'. At the age of twenty-five, he was called up and commenced a chequered career in the Pioneer Corps, being twelve times convicted for going absent and finally discharged on psychiatric grounds with 'anxiety state'. At that time he was complaining of sleeplessness, headaches and various bodily pains. He had a persistent twitching of the face, and was tense and fidgety. On account of a sore throat accompanied by similar nervous complaints he had once been admitted to hospital as a suspected case of meningitis, but was discharged within a week with a diagnosis of tonsillitis. His subsequent work record was notable for innumerable changes of job due to frequent stopping off from work with headaches and blackouts which he attributed to the after-effects of meningitis. He said that he could not bear noise, or working in closed rooms. Such conditions would make him irritable and he would have to walk out.

In spite of superior intelligence (I.Q. 120), he had been in trouble for petty thieving all his life, commencing with a first conviction at the age of thirteen, progressing through Borstal training and repeated imprisonments, until he arrived at preventive detention after his seventeenth conviction, on which occasion the charges involved a total sum of less than five pounds. He said he started thieving as a child out of sheer devilment when he was one of the delinquent gang.

In this example, as in many other cases, the man's neurotic complaints were inextricably interwoven with generalised inadequacy of personality and poor social performance. It was not that he had particular conflicts about employment, or marriage, or sex, although he was in fact grossly maladjusted in all these respects, but rather that he could not withstand stress on any front. He had two stock responses in the face of difficulty, either a collapse into neurotic invalidism, or a desperately petulant hitting back in the form of stupid, ineffectual crimes. Among the inadequates, especially, these two types of response-pattern frequently coexisted in the same individual.

4. Sexual Disorders

The prevalence of serious sexual disorders provided another indication of psychiatric morbidity. The incidence among these prisoners was much greater than would appear from the presence of five men serving sentences for sexual offences. Of the five convicted sex offenders, three had been sentenced for homosexual practices. All three had deep inhibitions which prevented sexual contacts with women. At least two other men (25, 72) had a similar trouble, although they had never been brought to court for their homosexual activities. A further three (4, 52, 97) confessed to homosexual inclinations in addition to heterosexual interests. One of these (97) was known by the police to be in the habit of making contact with homosexuals at Turkish baths for the purpose of stealing from them. Another two prisoners, both among the psychotic cases, were preoccupied with thinly disguised homosexual fantasies. A third psychotic was known to be a fetishist. Another man (35), described in a police report as 'a self-confessed sodomite', denied homosexuality but admitted practising self-flagellation while dressed in women's underwear. One man (63) was a compulsive exhibitionist, another (77) described sado-masochistic habits, and yet another (90) complained — somewhat unconvincingly — of a revulsion against the idea of sexual intercourse. Many of the single men were reported by their relatives never to have had girl-friends or to have shown much interest in women. In these cases it was virtually impossible to tell whether this behaviour was the result of specifically sexual disorder or whether it was just another manifestation of generalised social ineffectiveness and isolation. Some men spoke as if their interest in the opposite sex had dried up many years ago.

In a recent study of Borstal youths, T. C. N. Gibbens[1] comments: 'The main general characteristic of the heterosexual behaviour of the delinquent seems to be this tendency to "lose interest" — a constantly recurring phrase. These late adolescents tend to have a history of early promiscuity or mixed friendships; little by little their friends drift away with steady girl-friends and the gang become increasingly composed of somewhat desperate youths who have no physical or social sexual contacts. . . .' In other words, the delinquent starts off sexually normal — if not somewhat advanced — but his inability to sustain social or personal relationships interferes with sexual maturation. The impression given by some of these older prisoners confirms this view. Although normally heterosexual in orientation, many men said they 'don't bother'

[1] Gibbens, T. C. N., 'The Sexual Behaviour of Young Criminals', *Journ. Mental Science*, 1957, 103, 527–40.

about girls except perhaps for fleeting contacts with prostitutes or casual 'pick ups' which their relatives would not know about. The following comment (99) sums up the attitude expressed by many of the single men:

> 'I could have been married a long time ago, especially in the war, but I didn't seem interested. . . . I haven't been with any women — never lived with one. Just odd nights. Never had a woman friend for a long time. I'm not highly sexed. I can do without it. Outside too I can forget all about it. Just the same as beer. I never touch it outside.'

If they did not bring up the matter spontaneously, most of the preventive detainees were asked about their attitudes to homosexuality. An open-ended question, such as 'What about sex with men?', was put to them during a part of the interview when sexual matters were discussed. Apart from the two men who were convicted homosexual offenders, the question was raised with forty of the preventive detainees. A half of them described homosexual activities as taking place in prison, and only one positively denied any knowledge of such occurrences (67). None of them, however, was prepared to admit to participation himself. A quarter of them expressed vigorously condemnatory attitudes, e.g.:

> 'It turns my stomach. I'd have nothing to do with it . . . rife in these places . . . disgusting' (100).
>
> 'I detest that bloody business. I've no time for it. I'd burn the lot of them. I've met a lot [i.e. in prison] and I hate the sight of them' (94).
>
> 'Good lord, no! Not me! . . . It does happen, but I think it's revolting.'

A half were neutral or permissive:

> 'I speak to them but that's as far as it goes. They can't help being like that' (57).
>
> 'I've seen a lot of it, but I take no notice' (58).

VII

PSYCHOPATHIC TRAITS

1. Criteria of Psychopathy

One of the aims of this survey was to investigate the occurrence of the syndrome called psychopathic personality. This concept has had such a chequered history that some clinicians regard it as no more than a rag-bag of diagnostic left-overs, or as a simple term of abuse reflecting the mutual dislike of conventional psychiatrists and unco-operative members of the criminal classes. To this day no agreement exists as to the correct meaning of the term or the range of individuals to whom it should be applied. In effect, present standards vary so widely that of the prisoners examined practically every one or else none at all might be diagnosed as psychopathic.

The word has two broad usages. The first is as a synonym for personality deviation or sociopathy. In this sense the label applies to any individual whose character traits (however produced) deviate so far from the culturally accepted norm that he finds difficulty in conforming to ordinary social demands. Since this aspect had been discussed in a previous section, we can proceed to discuss the second usage of the word. This is a more traditional meaning and is better expressed by the old-fashioned terms 'constitutional inferiority' or 'moral imbecility'. The theory behind this usage envisages a class of unfortunates with an innate defect of feeling which prevents them from ever developing control over their brutish impulses or acquiring sensitivity to the needs of others besides themselves. The defect resembles the pathological varieties of mental subnormality, in which innate defects of cerebral equipment hinder mental growth. In the case of the psychopath, his defect is presumed to allow of the development of comprehension while preventing the development of conscience. Supposing the basis of both types of defect to consist of flaws in the genes, one might expect a certain overlap, and indeed one does find a proportion of mental defectives also exhibiting the amoral qualities of the psychopath.

Modern theorists have widened the scope of the term by

postulating other types of pathology, such as brain damage in childhood due to injury or infection. Gross deprivation of ordinary human warmth and affection at critical phases of development has also been put forward as a possible cause. Just as a child who is sufficiently isolated and neglected at a time when he should be learning to talk and to communicate may never catch up intellectually, so an unwanted and grossly rejected child may sustain permanent emotional damage. As has been suggested by McCord,[1] the essential element may be the combination of unfavourable environmental and physical factors, the presence of both simultaneously being necessary to the genesis of psychopathy.

This concept of psychopathy as a pathological state, probably resulting from severe trauma or inherent defect, rests upon clinical identification of a class of individuals exhibiting a characteristic combination of traits. This constellation or syndrome has been described again and again by generations of clinicians. In spite of changes of emphasis and terminology, they all seem to point to essentially the same entity. The fundamental features can be summed up as follows:

(1) A severe disturbance of behaviour in the absence of a psychotic or neurotic illness of sufficient severity to explain it.
(2) Liability to unrestrained, impulsive aggression at slight provocation.
(3) Anti-social behaviour suggestive of an inhuman indifference to other peoples' feelings.

The last-named item has been described in a bewildering variety of ways, as shallowness of affect, insincerity, lovelessness, lack of conscience, absence of guilt or remorse for harm done, and as semantic aphasia. The last curious phrase, which was used by Cleckley,[2] simply means that for the psychopath some humanitarian sentiments have no real meaning because he never actually experiences them. Like a tone-deaf person eulogising a musical composition, he may put on a show by mimicking other peoples' reactions, but his protestations remain a verbal exercise, devoid of genuine feeling.

Many subsidiary features are described in the literature. Inability to modify behaviour in the light of experience, lack of

[1] McCord, W. and McCord, J., *Psychopathy and Delinquency*, New York, 1956.
[2] Cleckley, H., *The Mask of Sanity*, St Louis, 1950.

foresight, heedlessness of painful consequences, living on the impulse of the moment and intolerance of frustration receive frequent mention. They have not been given prominence in the present classification because most of them seem to be derived from, or to be different ways of describing, the three fundamental elements already enumerated.

The components of the psychopathic syndrome consist of patterns of behaviour which manifest when the psychopath has to deal with other people in real-life situations. Responses to an interviewing psychiatrist provide indications of what happens elsewhere, but the best evidence comes from the life history and the testimony of relatives or others who have watched the man's reactions over years. For this reason particular importance was attached to the social history when making assessments of psychopathic traits.

In this investigation problems of causation were deliberately set aside and answers sought to two relatively simple questions. First, what proportion of habitual prisoners actually fit the textbook description of a psychopath, as just outlined? Second, do the traits which comprise the syndrome usually appear together, in full force, and in easily identifiable form, or do they more often occur in isolation and in varying degrees of development? The answer to this second question has an obvious bearing upon whether psychopaths belong to a class of their own, or whether they should be thought of as just an extreme example of the personality deviation common to numbers of recidivists.

Only the preventive detainees were investigated from the outset specifically with a view to the elucidation of psychopathic traits, so the systematic assessments and rating scales about to be described apply only to them, but the group of intermittent recidivists were in many ways similar, and the information about them was sufficient to provide for some impressionistic comparisons.

At interviews with the preventive detainees and their relatives the investigators had by them a form listing a series of traits associated with the psychopathic syndrome. These included: psychotic symptoms, neurotic tendency, impulsive aggression, inability to maintain relationships, insincere shallow feelings, boastfulness, persistent lying, freedom from guilt or remorse. The form actually contained more items, but several had to be abandoned as being too subjective or too difficult to assess. Against each item on the form were the figures 0, 1, 2, one of which had to be circled according to the absence, presence in a marked degree, or presence in an extreme degree, of the quality in question. The forms were filled up in the first instance independently after each prison interview or home visit. The two forms were later brought together and the final ratings decided upon after discussion. At the outset, long descriptive definitions of each of the items were written out in an attempt to preserve a uniform standard of marking. These had to be somewhat modified in the light of experience.

The first two items, psychotic symptoms and neurotic tendency, have already been discussed. The former were present in seven cases, the latter in a further twenty-four, of which nine were severely affected (score 2). Absence of mental symptoms, the first of the three criteria of psychopathy, was thus fulfilled by a residual minority of only nineteen cases out of fifty.

2. Impulsive Aggression

Impulsive aggression, the second criterion of the psychopathic syndrome, is commonly attributed to failure of social learning such that minor frustration provokes a primitive, childlike response of tantrums and violence.

In making the rating on this item attention was paid to evidence of outbursts of temper at slight provocation, whether expressed verbally or in blows. The standard of this and all other ratings was governed by the consideration that no one should be given a positive score who did not show the trait to a sufficiently unusual extent to be noticed by relatives (or by the hypothetical man-in-the-street) as an oddity. In this instance, isolated examples of loss of temper would carry no weight, but repeated outbursts, especially if of an explosive quality, or accompanied by violence out of proportion to the circumstances, were given a positive rating. Stories of incidents in youth, or under the age of thirty, provided they were not followed by similar episodes in later life, were ignored. Chronically irritable, disgruntled, suspicious or generally hostile characters were not rated as impulsively aggressive, unless they also had unrestrained outbursts. Aggressive behaviour during phases of active psychosis was also discounted.

As has been remarked already, the criminal records and the disciplinary records during imprisonment showed surprisingly little evidence of overt aggression among the preventive detainees, and further consideration of information given by their relatives served only to confirm that impression. Eight men were given scores of 1, but for most of this impulsive aggression was far from being their most prominent characteristic, in fact four of them were classed as predominantly passive-inadequate types in spite of their occasional outbursts. Only two cases (61, 88) showed impulsive aggressiveness to an extreme degree (score 2) such as might have qualified them for inclusion as psychopaths, but neither of them fulfilled the other criteria of psychopathy at all well. Here is one example:

Case 61

Aged forty-six, physically fit and of strong sturdy physique and average intelligence (I.Q. 95), this man was separated from his wife and also separated from the woman with whom he went to live with after leaving his wife. Convicted on twelve occasions, once for wounding, the remainder for offences of breaking and entering, he had had, in addition, four summary convictions for being drunk and disorderly and fighting. It was for an attack on the husband of the woman he was living with that he received his conviction for wounding. He had once been charged but acquitted following a knife fight in a fish and chip shop. He was regarded as dangerous by the police, and had on one occasion used a broken bottle to resist arrest. He mostly chose factories for breaking into, and was a daring climber in these exploits. On one occasion he fell through a roof and was concussed, but recovered sufficiently to crawl home. He explained that he felt 'all those factory padlocks a challenge', especially when he was in an irritable or 'fed-up' mood.

At interview he was somewhat aggressive and distinctly suspicious, and kept suggesting that the psychiatrist was in league with the police. He refused to allow any relatives to be seen. The description he gave of his upbringing rang true, but could not be checked. He said he was the middle of a family of thirteen, that his father had deserted in his infancy, and that he had had a bullying step-father since the age of eight. This seemed to leave the paternity of some of his siblings unexplained, but he was too aggressive for the point to be cleared up satisfactorily. He described his mother as doling out rough justice with a strap. His step-father, who also had a criminal record, used to kick him about, but he refused to knuckle under. At school he was good at sports, made friends readily, was rather adventurous and truanted persistently.

He was big for his age, and on starting work pretended to be older so as to get into a large firm in America. There he associated with older men of criminal habits, and was involved in armed robberies. After that he always chose his friends among criminals. He married a girl of sixteen who had a criminal brother, and later he cohabited with a woman with a criminal husband. He gave their sexual infidelity to him as a reason for leaving both these women. He admitted drinking habitually to excess. In spite of this, and of his previous imprisonments, he was a hard-working employee who had good recommendations from firms he had worked for.

3. Emotional Indifference

Behaviour suggestive of inhuman indifference to the feelings of others, which was put forward as the third criterion of psychopathy, was the one most difficult to define, to assess or to convert into a numerical rating. Three aspects of this quality were separately assessed on the rating forms, namely shallowness of feeling, absence of normal sense of guilt, and persistent lying.

Shallowness or insincerity of feeling is frequently quoted as an attribute that distinguishes the psychopath's characteristic disturbance of personal relationships from that found in neurotics. Broadly speaking, the neurotic is over-anxious and ineffective because he cares too much, but the psychopath, in spite of his ready protestations of friendship and concern, in the long run behaves as if he 'couldn't care less'. Thus, he may express all the most laudable sentiments of devotion to his wife, yet when she falls pregnant at an inconvenient moment he promptly deserts her. When occasion demands, the shallow-feeling psychopath behaves with the same falseness and disloyalty towards his closest intimates as he does to the victims from whom he obtains money by fraud. Pale reflections of this kind of behaviour occasionally percolated through during psychiatric interviews when a prisoner went through the motions of friendliness and pretended to unburden himself while all the time he was really working on a smoke-screen of glib and coldly calculated lies.

A few prisoners made no pretence to finer feelings but declared roundly that they were lone wolves who did not give a rap about anyone and wanted to stay that way. Such characters, provided their assertions went beyond mere bravado and seemed to represent a definite attitude, were also rated positively on shallow feelings. Thirteen of the preventive detainees were rated as extremely shallow (score 2) and a further ten as noticeably so (score 1).

Another well-known trait distinguishing the psychopath from the neurotic is a conspicuous absence of guilt or remorse in situations in which the average person would feel acutely sorry and ashamed. The unstable neurotic tortures himself with self-questionings and ideas of guilt, but the psychopath remains unruffled no matter what harm his actions have produced. Some of the prisoners were like this. They showed no remorse either for their offences or for any other aspects of their behaviour. They could forsake wife and children, deceive their friends, let people down everywhere, and still maintain their equanimity. Any questions of personal responsibility they parried with involved explanations purporting to show that others were to blame.

On the other hand, some prisoners, although they expressed no shame about being 'an honest thief', did seem to suffer pangs of conscience on other matters. Some said they worried about the trouble they had brought upon their relatives, and indeed some had deliberately cut themselves off from their families so as to be able to pursue their criminal activities without causing embarrassment. Such men were not regarded as showing any psychopathic lack of guilt. They had simply identified themselves with a subculture among whom certain forms of dishonesty are acceptable.

Thirdly, and finally, all the preventive detainees were rated for indiscriminate lying. In making this assessment, necessary lying for the purpose of evading detection was ignored, and positive ratings were given only for habitual lying in a wide range of circumstances. 'You never could believe a word he said', was a comment made again and again by relatives. Some of the lying was boastful, indicative of a need for self-aggrandisement or the expression of face-saving fantasies, but much of it seemed aimless. In some cases men lied persistently at interview in circumstances in which they stood to gain nothing and on matters which could be immediately disproved. Twenty-one of the preventive detainees were rated as indiscriminate liars to a gross degree (score 2), and a further eight were conspicuous liars (score 1).

Shallow feeling, guiltlessness, and lying were closely intermingled in most cases. Men without emotional commitments, who never get beyond half-hearted shallow relationships, and really 'couldn't care less' about others, naturally have no regret for harm done and no compunction about lying and deceiving. Among the fifty preventive detainees, nineteen showed none of these traits to any conspicuous degree, but fifteen showed all three simultaneously. Since the three traits appeared to reflect the single prime quality of emotional indifference, it seemed justifiable to add together each individual's scores to produce a total rating which varied from a minimum of zero to a maximum of six. On this scale, ten of the preventive detainees manifested emotional indifference to an extreme degree (score 5 or 6). The following examples show the scoring system in application. In both cases their lying went to absurd lengths, suggestive of the influence of some pathological compulsion:

Case 56

A man of forty-five, married but separated from his wife, with a total of fifteen convictions for offences of stealing or fraud. He was in the habit of obtaining cars on hire-purchase and disposing of them fraudulently.

At interview he talked very fluently and revealed superior intelligence. He was cheerful and uninhibited but wildly unreliable in his statements, which varied each time he was interviewed by a different person. Although willing to acknowledge his culpability in the abstract, he volunteered long, circumstantial narratives extenuating himself from responsibility for any particular offence. He blandly denied ever having been in the town where one of his latest offences was committed, although, as was discovered later, he had in fact given himself up to the police and confessed that particular episode. He expressed great bitterness towards his wife, accusing her of frequent infidelities, blaming her for his troubles, and stating that she was at present living with another man. Significantly, he refused to allow the social worker to visit his wife, although he agreed to visits being made to other relatives. Enquiries from the probation service and his father-in-law revealed that he had deserted his wife for long periods each time a child was born and made no attempt to support her or the children. In spite of this she was devoted to him and had several times taken him back. She was now living with her parents.

His father and sister were also seen. Both of them seemed fond of him, but they admitted he had always been a terrible liar, boasting and exaggerating beyond all reason. His father recalled that once when late for school he insisted to the teacher that he had been chased round the playground by a tiger, and would not withdraw the story when it was disbelieved.

They described him as a person of great self-confidence, who was always sure of getting what he wanted, and in fact generally succeeded in doing so. He could charm anyone if he wanted to — and people liked him very readily, until they realised he could not be trusted. Highly irresponsible, but always good tempered and easy going, he was never violent or quarrelsome. A great spendthrift, he loved smart clothes, good-looking women and large cars. Although a capable worker, he would never settle for long. Once he built up a successful business as a radio mechanic, but threw the whole thing over without warning after less than a year.

Ratings: Emotional indifference 6
Lying 2
Guiltlessness 2
Shallow feelings 2
Impulsive aggression 0

Case 58

A single man, aged forty-eight, of average intelligence and tall, muscular physique. Since the age of seventeen he had been repeatedly convicted for stealing, usually for stealing rather small sums.

At interview he appeared co-operative and keen to make a good impression. He gave an account of a somewhat idyllic upbringing and described in graphic detail his father's death at the wheel of his taxi and his mother's death, hastened by the worry of her son's imprisonment. He said his wife had deserted him and left his two children with an unsatisfactory guardian who would not answer his letters. He would welcome enquiries about his children, and was willing for his siblings to be visited.

Owing to the prisoner's vagueness as to their whereabouts, his relatives were traced only with difficulty. The parents were found to be both of them alive and well. The mother tearfully confirmed the prisoner's upbringing, and described how his father used to make a fuss of him and take him out in the taxi. She was at a loss to account for the difference between the prisoner and his seven younger siblings, all of whom had made happy marriages and were good workers. The prisoner would never settle down, however much the family tried to help. He was a terrible liar, and was in the habit of obtaining sympathy from strangers by telling them of his mother's cruelty. He used to write affectionate letters from prison to his mother promising to 'work himself to the bone' for her in future, but over the years she had slowly come to the conclusion that such words had no meaning for him, his protestations were empty and his behaviour always unchanged.

A probation officer who knew him well described how the prisoner had elicited the sympathetic friendship of three different women, one of whom he robbed, one of whom he attacked with malicious letters addressed to her family, and one of whom was his victim in a conviction for demanding money with a menacing letter. It was found that he had never been married, and the alleged guardian of his children proved to be the wife of a fellow prisoner. She had visited him in prison as a kindness to her husband's friend, and he had retaliated by making trouble for her, saying she had stolen from him and causing visitors to call to claim her children as his own.

Following apprehension for his latest offence, he wrote a number of spiteful letters to people with whom he had recently been in contact, including one to the couple in whose house he had lodged. In this he alleged he had had sexual intercourse with the landlady. The letter provoked a double tragedy, suicide and attempted murder.

The prisoner was seen a second time and told of the visit to his parents. He was not at all put out. 'I thought they must be dead,' he remarked, 'because I haven't heard from them for so long.' Pressed about other points, he was equally off-hand. Asked what he felt about the tragedy to his former landlady he professed ignorance and complete disinterest. Finally he became slightly sulky and commented, 'I don't need friends or anyone. I can get on in the world without mixing with people. I'd sooner be on my own any day.'

Ratings: Emotional indifference 6
Shallowness 2
Guiltlessness 2
Lying 2
Impulsive aggression 0

Table 18 sets out the scores allotted to each individual case. In order to facilitate comparisons between traits, neurotic tendency and passive inadequacy[1] were also scored 0, 1, or 2 on three-point scales similar to those used for other traits. A glance at the table suffices to show that none of the preventive detainees fulfilled all three criteria, that is, absence of psychiatric symptoms, extreme impulsive aggressivity and extreme emotional indifference. The man who came nearest (94) fell short because he had only a moderate degree of impulsive aggression:

Case 94

A single man of fifty-six. His father had been a prosperous travelling showman, and he was reared in an affectionate but rather lax atmosphere, living in caravans among circus performers. His mother died when he was about six, but was replaced by an affectionate nannie who became his step-mother.

He was a rebellious, problem child from his earliest years. He truanted persistently, got up to all kinds of mischief about the fair-ground, stole persistently, from his home and from shops. His brother described him as 'a terrible liar, you can't believe a word'. His step-mother said he had roamed and truanted and defied his parents

[1] One borderline case of mixed attitudes (36), who was not predominantly an inadequate and had not been included in that class, was nevertheless given a positive score on this rating.

always. Reprimands and punishments left him completely unmoved and undeterred. His father was for ever rescuing him from the consequences of his actions. On one occasion his father found him pretending to be crippled and begging money. On another occasion he called at ice-cream stalls, pretending to represent the owner, and collected their rents. These exploits seemed pointless, because he had plenty of pocket money from his indulgent father. He also had plenty of attention, for he was clever at learning a turn for the shows, but he could never be relied upon to be at hand when wanted.

As he grew older, his exploits extended. His father made repeated efforts to co-operate with rehabilitation following approved school and Borstal committals, by providing him with a stable home and trying to pin him down to a regular place of employment, but the prisoner preferred to wander about the country living on his wits. At one point, while selling animals by trick, he passed himself off as a well-known naturalist, and on another occasion he pretended to be the son of a Hollywood film director.

His lively manner and glib tongue won him friends easily, but having no sense of loyalty he soon lost them again. He liked to have a girl for sexual intercourse, he said, but he would not dream of having one to live with him. During his service career he betrayed to enemy guards some fellow prisoners of war, who hoped to escape. They were shot. During one of his sentences of imprisonment he made a demonstrative attempt to hang himself. He told the psychiatrist he had done this because he was angry with some prison officers and hoped by this means to get them into trouble with their superiors for not supervising him sufficiently closely.

He was of average intelligence on testing, but a stupid boaster. He had once been convicted for wearing an officer's uniform and medals to which he was not entitled. When interviewed he boasted that he was the best card manipulator of all British conjurors, and also claimed to be an expert at safe blowing at a distance by radio control. Although trying to maintain a façade of contrition, he could not resist describing with relish the details of some of his more successful swindles.

About his plans on leaving prison he said, 'I'll just leave it to the gods. I want to get something someone else hasn't got. I'd like my own business — something new.'

He told the psychiatrist that a friend of his, who was a medical practitioner, had advised him that he needed treatment, perhaps a leucotomy operation, if ever he was to make an adjustment outside of prison. He said he felt this was absolutely correct, and he was keen to undergo any treatment necessary. The prison medical officer commented that this prisoner would be unlikely to co-operate in attending at any clinic or hospital once he gained his liberty. In fact, as the date of his release approached, he wrote to his medical friend that he had decided he was not a 'nut case' and did not want to go into a mental hospital. Within three months of release he was back in prison serving another and longer sentence of preventive detention.

4. Inter-relations between Traits

Fairly clear answers to the two questions posed at the outset have now emerged. First, not a single man among the preventive detainees fitted all the classical criteria of a psychopath. Second, the main constituents of the psychopathic syndrome manifested to a considerable extent separately and independently and in varying degrees of severity. Only exceptionally did they coincide all in the same individual to produce an approximation to the classical syndrome. Of the two main positive phenomena of psychopathy, the severer degrees of impulsive aggression hardly occurred at all, and emotional indifference, although relatively common, appeared largely independently and often in individuals who showed no trace of violence. As regards the first criterion, absence of psychiatric symptoms, this also was to some degree independent. Those with psychotic symptoms showed no lesser incidence of emotional indifference, and although the more florid examples of neurotic tendency and emotional indifference occurred, with one exception, in different individuals, slighter degrees quite often overlapped (see Table 19). These results fail to support the theory that psychopathic indifference invariably implies a bland denial of symptoms or conflicts. The suggestion that the two may often co-exist is not without precedent. In a recent follow-up study of 842 psychiatric cases among American servicemen R. L. Jenkins[1] reported: 'In this material it became very clear to all three raters that there is no contradiction in having both severe psycho-neurotic symptoms and severe psychopathic behaviour.' Of twenty-seven men who showed moderate or severe psychopathic features, twenty also showed moderate or severe psychoneurotic symptoms.

As has already been pointed out, psychiatric symptoms occurred most frequently among the passive-inadequates (see Table 12). Emotional indifference, on the other hand, occurred noticeably less often among the inadequates (see Table 20). Thus, in spite of the overlap just mentioned, the division into passively-inadequate

[1] Jenkins, R. L., 'The Psychopathic or Anti-social Personality', *Journ. Nervous and Mental Diseases*, 1960, 131, 318–34.

and actively anti-social prisoners did to some extent correspond to a division between worrying, symptom-complaining (neurotic) prisoners and emotionally indifferent (psychopathic) prisoners.

The connection between passive inadequacy and the commission of petty crimes of an unplanned character has already been discussed. Another connection between type of crime and personality traits was found among false pretenders in whom the quality of emotional indifference was especially prominent. The necessarily superficial and deceptive nature of the contacts established with their prospective victims seemed to pervade all their personal relationships. Of the twelve preventive detainees whose convictions (in the majority of their adult appearances at Court) involved charges of fraud or false pretences, seven had very high scores (i.e. 5 or 6) and the remainder had substantial positive scores (2, 3 or 4) on emotional indifference.

The findings discussed in this section so far apply only to preventive detainees, and since these were a noticeably docile group of prisoners it is a reasonable assumption that a different group might yield a higher proportion of true psychopaths. Re-inspection of the records of the fifty intermittent recidivists with this in mind amply confirmed the co-existence of mental symptoms and psychopathic traits, and also the relative independence of the incidence of impulsive violence and emotional indifference. There was, however, a distinctly higher incidence of impulsive aggression, and some eight cases might have been rated 2 on this count. Also, a few more cases came nearer than any of the preventive detainees to fulfilling all three criteria of psychopathy. To end this section, here are two final examples, taken from the intermittent recidivists, which represents the closest approximation to the classic psychopathic syndrome to be found among the whole hundred prisoners:

Case 3

A married man of thirty-seven, convicted on seven occasions for larceny, once for breach of probation and once for indecent exposure. His criminal record showed a gap of six years, from 1948 to 1954, but he admitted that he had 'never gone completely straight' during that time, and his wife, who was interviewed, mentioned that he used to provide extra money, which she was suspicious about, especially as she from time to time discovered discarded purses and handbags in her dustbin. He used to tell her he had earned extra doing overtime or that he had borrowed from a friend. She checked one of these stories and found it to be untrue.

The prisoner was born abroad. A slightly build man with traces of negroid physique and complexion, he was at first excitedly aggressive, and talked wildly about his wrongs and the maltreatment he was receiving. 'If this [interview] is compulsory I shall put in a petition to the Home Office; if not, then I don't want to answer any questions.' He was eventually placated somewhat by a promise to obtain news of his children, who had been taken into care by the local authority, and he agreed to see the psychiatrist again (the first interview having been entirely taken up by complaints and threatened reprisals against the authorities). In the course of two further interviews, he produced a life story which it was not possible to substantiate. (He had given his wife a somewhat different story, which she did not believe.) He also let the psychiatrist see his autobiography, which he had written with a view to publication, and which he said was worth £2,500. This consisted of a highly dramatised story of the cruelties suffered by a young boy at the hands of a wicked aunt, who was his guardian, and the solace he received from another child, his female cousin. The pair became romantic lovers, and the boy tried to prove his worth by acts of bravery at sea. The whole work was excessively childish, both in style and feeling, and certainly represented a dream-like fantasy far removed from the sordid facts of his real life.

He had married while serving in the forces during the war. She had been his pen-friend. At interview, she said the prisoner was insatiable in his sexual demands, and was frequently unfaithful to her. On one occasion, a woman turned up at the house saying she was his fiancée and was astounded to find he already had a wife and family. The wife gave a fair picture of the prisoner's peculiarities. She said he liked to work, but seldom kept a job for long as he usually got annoyed with his employer and then left. Six months was about the longest he had ever kept a job. He was always boastful, and liked to 'act big'. Once, while in the forces, he received twenty-eight days' detention for wearing medals to which he was not entitled. He squandered money on making a show for his friends, but he never seemed to keep friends for long. He liked his wife to wear exotic hair styles to impress people. He was of violent and unpredictable temper, jealously inclined and easily offended. The wife said she was not really afraid of him, although he often struck her, but he terrorised the children. He had also smashed all their furniture in one of his rages. She felt he was completely self-centred and not truly interested in the family. Eventually she deserted with the lodger, taking with her three of their six children. She heard later that the ones left behind were being bullied and victimised by the prisoner.

At interviews the prisoner spoke with satisfaction of having behaved like a martinet to his children, locking them up all day without food, and giving his eldest boy 'a beating he'll never forget' when he found him smoking a cigarette. (The boy was subsequently committed to an approved school). He fulminated against his wife for her infidelity, and complained that she had always been appallingly dirty and untidy. (The state of the home and children when the wife was visited, without previous notice, suggested quite the contrary.) He was preoccupied with ideas of revenge, and of regaining control of his children so as to be able to tell them all about their mother's wickedness. In this, as in other matters, he revealed a childishly spiteful attitude and a lack of real concern for his childrens' welfare. His aggressive attitudes were partly histrionic. He said: 'If I meet up with that man [i.e. his wife's lover] outside, I'll be in the death cell next time.' Also: 'If I don't get the children back I'll play havoc with society.' He had in fact created a scene in the Juvenile Court when he was refused custody of the children He had visited the Children's Officer, lost his temper with her and threatened to murder her. In spite of similar aggressive attitudes when first seen for this enquiry he calmed down dramatically once interest was taken in his autobiographical MS, and said ingratiatingly, 'I'm not such a bad chap as they make me out to be.'

He complained a lot about 'terrible headaches' due to migraine which the prison authorities declined to treat, but when questioned about these his descriptions became vague. It was clear that the symptoms did not interfere with his sleep or appetite, caused no disturbance of vision, and were almost certainly hysterical.

Case 36

A divorced man aged fifty-two with a record of eight convictions, including one charge of arson and one of malicious damage.

He came of a normal working-class family. His siblings had all done well, and the family had made great efforts to help him out of his many troubles. He had been a problem ever since babyhood, when he had screaming fits and could not bear noises. His mother described a serious fall on his head in infancy, when he was at first thought to have been killed.

Throughout his childhood he remained a problem, truanting, lying and stealing, and failing to make friends. The pattern persisted when he started work. He was repeatedly dismissed after quarrels, thefts or failure to carry out his duties. In the army he was a complete misfit, stole from fellow soldiers, and complained he acted under some impulse he could not control. He was discharged on psychiatric grounds.

In personality he was highly sensitive, moody, reserved, quarrelsome and impulsive. When things went well he could be pleasant and agreeable and show affection for his family, but if crossed in any way he was liable to rages, to steal or to become destructive, and to wander off on his own, later presenting himself at police stations or hospitals claiming he had 'lost his memory'. He was curiously accident prone, and had had an unusual number of quite severe injuries at work and elsewhere.

He had been many times admitted for short periods to observation wards or mental hospitals. At the age of thirty-two he began a long stay, of some seven years, for the most part as a certified patient. While in hospital he was thought to be devoid of social responsibility, plausible and ingratiating, but a persistent thief, and quite untrustworthy. On one occasion he nearly strangled another patient, a feeble defective boy, in an unprovoked attack, but afterwards he showed no adequate remorse or appreciation of the seriousness of what he had done. At times he talked to fellow patients or prisoners of other killings he had committed, and he was actually suspected and questioned by the police.

At interviews for this research, he showed no defect of reasoning, but gave the most blood-curdling descriptions of his violence in a quiet, matter-of-fact, unruffled tone. Immediately previous to his latest imprisonment he had been living with a woman who was a partially recovered paranoid schizophrenic.

This last case was about the only example in the whole series of a man prone to irrational, dangerous and unpredictable violence. His wildly unstable behaviour was probably at least in part the result of brain injury.

VIII

PSYCHOLOGICAL TESTS AND CLINICAL FINDINGS

1. The Tests Used

The estimates of passive-inadequacy and emotional indifference, which constituted the two most important personality variables identified by clinical observation, were based entirely upon subjective judgement and are therefore open to the criticism that they might measure the observer's prejudices more than the prisoners' real characteristics. It is an advantage to have some independent measure with which to compare these clinical assessments, both as a protection against the effects of personal bias and as a means of exploring further the nature of the variables in question.

Dr J. G. Field administered a considerable number of psychological tests to all of the preventive detainees. Only those three tests which one might expect to prove most closely relevant are considered here, namely, the *Minnesota Multiphasic Personality Inventory*, the *Maudsley Personality Inventory*, and a tactile conditioning test. Both of the inventories are self-rating questionnaires. The *Minnesota Inventory* asks subjects to sort into groups of true or false — as applied to themselves — a series of propositions such as:

At times I think I am no good at all.
At times I feel like smashing things.
I find it hard to make talk when I meet people.

The *Maudsley Personality Inventory* calls for responses of yes, no or doubtful to a series of questions such as:

Are there times when you cannot bear the company of anyone?

The responses to each inventory can be scored according to a variety of scales. The expected scores for average persons, and the range of variation in an ordinary population, are public knowledge. For this research, the *Maudsley Personality Inventory* was scored for responses indicative of 'neuroticism', 'extraversion' and 'lying'. For example, the item 'Do you like to mix socially with people?' is included in this scale and contributes 2, 1 or 0 points to the score of 'extraversion' according to whether the response is 'yes', '?' or 'no' respectively. High scores on the scale of extraversion are supposed to differentiate persons who tend to be outgoing and sociable, interested in outside happenings more than their own feelings or motivations.

The 'lie scale' on the *Maudsley Personality Inventory* consists of items such as:

Do you sometimes talk about things you know nothing about?
Do you sometimes get cross?
Do you sometimes put off until tomorrow what you ought to do today?

Most persons, if they are truthful, answer yes to these items, if they answer no this contributes two points to their score on the lie scale. Thus, high scorers on this scale tend to be persons who lie in the direction of making exaggerated claims to moral perfection.

The neuroticism scale includes such items as:

Do you often experience periods of loneliness?
Have you often lost sleep over your worries?
Would you rate yourself as a tense or 'high strung' individual?

An affirmative reply contributes two points. High scorers on this scale tend to be persons of anxious, neurotic temperament, prone to react with mental symptoms or 'breakdowns' when under stress.

In order for these scores to provide meaningful information, the subject must be at least sufficiently co-operative and attentive not to give just random responses. Extreme and systematic untruthfulness will also to some extent invalidate the scores. For example, a person who has a high 'lie score', one who tends to falsify his answers so as to present a too favourable picture of himself, may also falsely deny some of the unfavourable sounding items on the neuroticism scale, and so produce an unduly low score on neuroticism. This did in fact happen. Among the ten prisoners who produced abnormally high lie scores (i.e. over twenty) were several who also produced very low, and certainly false neuroticism scores. Expressed more precisely, the twelve prisoners who had the lowest neuroticism scores included nine of the ten prisoners with the highest lie scores. The lying which resulted in a high lie score on the questionnaire was of a particular kind and in the context of a special situation. The correspondence with indiscriminate lying, as rated by the psychiatrist, was only slight and obtained only for those individuals who produced really high lie scores (see Table 21). Two cases (56 and 58, see pp. 67–8 and 68–9) were earlier cited in this report as instances of lying carried to ridiculous lengths. Both of these were among the ten individuals who gave the highest lie scores. These ten individuals also included three of the seven psychotic cases. These same three psychotics (18, 34, 35) were among the six lowest scorers on the neuroticism scale. These results suggest that very high lie scores might provide an easy means of identifying among prisoners some of the pathological liars and some of the psychotics.

The *Minnesota Multiphasic Personality Inventory* was scored according to five scales known as the Psychopathic deviate (Pd) scale, the Psychaesthenia scale (Pt), the Hysteria scale (Hy), the Validity score (F) and the Correction score (K). The last two scales are similar to the lie score on the *Maudsley Personality Inventory* in that they give some indication of the truthfulness or validity of the subjects responses. To quote the instruction manual to the test: 'A high K score represents defensiveness against psychological weakness, and may indicate a defensiveness that verges upon deliberate distortion in the direction of making a more "normal" appearance.' Not surprisingly, the three psychotic men (78, 84, 95) who produced very low neuroticism scores and very high lie scores on the *Maudsley Inventory* were among the nine highest scorers on this scale. These men pursued a consistent policy of denial of symptoms. On the whole, however, the group did not produce unusual K scores, and although scatter diagrams were prepared and carefully scrutinised, no relationships between K scores and the psychiatric variables were detectable.

To quote the manual again: 'If the F score is high, the other scales are likely to be invalid, either because the subject was careless or unable to comprehend the items, or because extensive scoring or recording errors were made.' If an individual scores more than twelve on the F scale, and fifteen of the fifty prisoners did so, his scores on the other scales are generally regarded as invalid.

The *Minnesota Inventory* presents subjects with a rather more difficult task than the *Maudsley Inventory*. It has many more items, 550 in all, and the wording is sometimes rather more complicated. This may have contributed to the number of high scores on the

F scale. The F scale includes items about delusional ideas, such as: 'I believe I am being plotted against'; 'Someone has been trying to poison me'. Such items, if claimed as applicable, raise the F score. A tendency to exaggerate symptoms, or claim non-existent symptoms, also raises the F score. For this reason, F scores tend to correlate negatively with scores on the Maudsley lie scale. They certainly did so in this instance. For some reason, possibly because of their tendency to make the most of their complaints, the passive inadequates showed a significant tendency to produce high F scores (see Table 24). The number of cases was too small to allow of the elimination of all fifteen high F scorers. In the analyses which follow, they are, however, considered separately, so as to see if their contribution made any difference to the trends observed.

2. Neuroticism and Extraversion

As already reported by Dr Field[1] the scores on the neuroticism scale achieved by preventive detainees were significantly and consistently higher in average ($27{\cdot}70 \pm 12{\cdot}25$, $N = 150$) than control groups of normal individuals. ($21{\cdot}41 \pm 10{\cdot}34$ for 80 apprentices. $19{\cdot}89 \pm 11{\cdot}02$ for 55 'normal' persons.) This result suggests that preventive detainees in general include a substantial number of persons of marked neurotic tendency, a proposition entirely in conformity with the psychiatric findings already described.

The figures showed an association between passive inadequacy as rated by the psychiatrist and neuroticism as assessed by the questionnaire (see Table 22). Excluding the ten cases with very high lie scores, whose neuroticism scores were correspondingly unreliable, the association becomes clearer. Only a third of those not classed as inadequates, compared with three-quarters of those classed as extremely inadequate, have high neuroticism scores (i.e. scores exceeding those of fifty per cent of the individuals tested). Although the figures are small the trend is obvious, statistically significant, and in conformity with that already noted by clinical comparisons.

The psychaesthenia (Pt) scale is a very similar measure to the Maudsley neuroticism scale. It seeks to identify persons of a basically anxious temperament, prone to unreasonable fears or compulsive behaviour. The scores on this scale did in fact

[1] Field, J. G., Report to the Prison Commissioners on an Investigation into the Personality of Recidivists, July 1960, unpublished. 'Two Types of Recidivist . . .', *Brit. Journ. Criminol.*, 1962, 3, 377–81.

differentiate effectively those classed as inadequate, who tended to score highly (see Table 25). The relationship was due entirely to the fact that the highest scorers on this scale were also the highest scorers on the F scale,[1] the one which identifies persons who give unreliable answers. This curious result was probably due to the tendency, on the part of the passive inadequates, to exaggerate any complaints or symptoms, which tendency would be liable to produce a high F score and a high Pt score simultaneously.

The results of the Pt scale also bore some relation to magnitude of offences. The six individuals who had attempted to acquire the largest amounts in dishonest gains (i.e. values over £300 in the main charges at their latest conviction) all scored low (i.e. less than fifteen) on this scale. This constitutes some slight evidence in favour of the clinical impression that the more enterprising criminals are also the least neurotic.

According to theoretical expectations, criminals, and especially 'psychopaths', tend towards extraversion more than the population at large. The scores suggest that this generalisation does not extend to preventive detainees. Dr Field reported (*ibid*) an average score on the extraversion scale of 24·27 ± 8·41 for 150 preventive detainees, which was very close to the average of 24·91 ± 0·71 obtained with a control group of 1800 'normals'.

The degree of extraversion, as measured by the *Maudsley Personality Inventory*, did correlate significantly with the psychiatric rating of emotional indifference. (Product moment $r = 0{\cdot}30$, $P < 0{\cdot}05$). Three-quarters of those with high ratings on emotional indifference (i.e. 4, 5 or 6) compared with only one-third of those with low ratings (score 0 or 1) produced scores indicative of tendency to extraversion (i.e. exceeding the scores of fifty per cent of those tested) (see Table 23). This result confirms that the more 'psychopathic' prisoners, those with extreme emotional indifference, do tend to be predominantly extraverted individuals. Since these 'psychopathic' types were in the minority, they did not produce a trend towards extraversion among preventive detainees in general. There was also a suggestive association between passive inadequacy and relative introversion. Only thirty-eight per cent of other types compared with 58·6 per cent of those classed as 'inadequates' gave scores on the introverted side of the scale, i.e. exceeded by fifty per cent of those tested.

[1] The sixteen prisoners with the highest Pt scores (thirteen of them inadequates) included fourteen out of fifteen highest F scorers.

The hysteria scale (Hy) of the *Minnesota* test purports to identify persons who are liable to develop physical symptoms in response to stress. The items include a series of statements about complaints such as:

'Much of the time my head seems to hurt all over.'

The scores produced on this scale correlated significantly with clinical ratings of liability to psychiatric symptoms, and also with the ratings of passive-inadequacy ($P<0{\cdot}01$), but there was no association with emotional indifference (see Table 25). The general trend was not affected in either instance by the elimination of the fifteen cases with F score over 12.

The association between 'psychiatric symptoms' and test scores was closer on this scale than on either the *Maudsley* 'neuroticism' or the *Minnesota* 'Psychaesthenia' scales. This was probably because the Hy items and the psychiatric ratings were more concerned with actual complaints than with latent anxiety.

The psychopathic deviate (Pd) scale of the *Minnesota Inventory* was also scored. High scores on this scale are produced by 'a group of persons whose main difficulty lies in their absence of deep emotional response, their inability to profit from experience, and their disregard of social mores'. The following are examples of relevant items:

'In school I was sometimes sent to the Principal for cutting up.'
'During one period when I was a youngster I engaged in petty thievery.'
'My parents have often objected to the kind of people I went around with.'

To address such queries to a group of men known to have been persistently at loggerheads with the law is admittedly tautological. Nevertheless, the fact that prisoners, this group included, produce significantly higher scores than 'normals' suggests at least a certain degree of candour in their responses to questionnaires. Scores on this scale did not, however, differentiate between individuals rated low and high on 'emotional difference', or between those rated by the psychiatrist as 'indiscriminate' liars and 'non-liars', or to any significant degree between 'inadequates' and 'others' (see Table 27). The four individuals classed as relatively normal, 'non-deviant' personalities all scored low on this scale. One may tentatively conclude that this scale, while of some use in distinguishing between criminals and non-criminals, is less useful for distinguishing one kind of criminal from another.

3. Conditioning Tests

No relationships whatsoever were discovered between scores on tactile conditioning and any of the psychiatric ratings, so this test need be mentioned only very briefly. The test is a measure of the ease or difficulty with which conditioned responses can be established in an individual. In this instance, the stimulus used was a puff of air directed towards the eye, accompanied by a noise of controlled duration, intensity and tone. The test results were based upon the number of times the noise-puff combination had to be repeated in order to make the subject blink automatically to noise alone. According to theory, individuals in whom conditioned responses are established only with difficulty are persons who learn less easily the responses expected of them in social situations. On this theory, criminals would be expected to give low scores on conditioning tests.[1]

Dr Field found that this theoretical prediction was not confirmed by the scores of the fifty-one preventive detainees, which were in general similar to those obtained from a group of normal persons. He suggested that perhaps the prisoners included two groups, the bad learners or 'psychopaths', who had never acquired adequate social responses, and the good learners who had been subjected to bad social influences and therefore learned the wrong pattern. On this hypothesis, Dr Field predicted that the poor-conditioners or 'psychopaths' would come from relatively good homes, since theirs was a disturbance peculiar to themselves, whereas the good conditioners would come from bad homes, since their anti-social habits were the outcome of social pressures.

The predicted trend did not in fact appear. As will be described later, the prisoners' upbringings were classified into four categories, from good to very bad. The discipline they had experienced in their parental homes was also classified into normal, lax and/or casual, inconsistent, and harsh and/or over-strict. Neither of these classifications showed any clear association with scores obtained on the conditioning tests.

[1] Field, J. G. and Brengleman, J. C., 'Eyelid Conditioning and Three Personality Parameters,' *Journ. Abnormal Soc. Psychol.*, 1961, 63, 517–23.

This single negative result does not, of course, provide an adequate test of the theory. Conditioning is a complex process, and conditioning of one special response in a particular situation may not reflect accurately conditioning in a wider context.

4. Test Results and Clinical Classifications

Recapitulating the main positive findings, comparisons between scores on personality tests and independent clinical assessments revealed some statistically significant correlations. The clinical assessments must therefore have reflected something more than prejudice in the observer. Two of the chief clinical observations, namely the high incidence of neurotic tendency and the positive association between this and passive-inadequacy, were both confirmed. In addition, the clinical ratings of emotional indifference were found to be positively correlated with the test measurement of extraversion. The findings lent some support to the clinical division between passive-inadequates and active-aggressive or predatory types of anti-social personality, the former group including a higher proportion of introverted and neurotic individuals, the latter with a higher proportion of extraverted and emotionally indifferent individuals. Among subsidiary points of interest was confirmation of the presence of a number of pathological liars, some confirmation of the suggestion that the more enterprising criminals were among the least neurotic, and also some indications that the passive-inadequates tend to exaggerate their neurotic complaints.

The clinical ratings were made with a view to classification for the purpose of choosing between various methods of control or treatment. The fact that personality tests which were not specially designed for this purpose yielded correlating results suggests that, given some development and refinement, such tests might provide a practical guide in the allocation of prisoners to varying regimes.

IX

FAMILY BACKGROUNDS RECONSIDERED

1. Classification of Backgrounds

Researches based upon young persons who have become established criminals yield, with depressing regularity, a stereotyped picture of social disorder firmly rooted in chaotic family background and manifestly unsatisfactory upbringing. A high proportion are found to be the unwanted products of disunited or broken marriages and to have been subjected as children to serious mishandling in the form of cruelty, rejection, neglect or inconsistency. It seems plausible to suppose that the worst among such cases, those whose characters have been twisted beyond hope of reform, should be the ones to go on to become confirmed recidivists in later life. Even so, it does not follow that the group of older habitual prisoners should be composed exclusively of men from bad homes who started as juvenile delinquents and went steadily from bad to worse. The fact that a substantial proportion have never had convictions as juveniles suggests a different picture.

Factors unrelated to delinquent behaviour contribute to the absence of juvenile records. Some of the more elderly prisoners passed their adolescence before courts reserved for juveniles came into operation and in times when children were less often arraigned. For various reasons, such as the destruction of old files, the official criminals records are unlikely to be always complete in this respect. In theory, the juvenile courts record findings of guilt, not criminal convictions, the idea being that records of childhood should not be preserved for use against the well-behaved adult. However, policy with respect to the destruction of old records seems rather inconsistent, and such factors do not provide a complete explanation of the apparent frequency of late entry into crime. Regardless of what may have happened to them as juveniles, many older recidivists do not appear at adult courts until their mid-twenties.

Most of the prisoners in this series talked freely about their recollections of childhood. Special attention was paid to these particulars and efforts were made to obtain confirmation from relatives or other sources. Although the information was sometimes sketchy and unreliable, because prisoners were untruthful or relatives ageing, inaccessible or otherwise poor informants, nevertheless it was possible to form a broad impression of the outstanding features of family background in most instances. Sufficient information was available on all of the preventive detainees and on 43 of the intermittent recidivists to supply a rough grading of the family backgrounds.

Cases were allotted to one or other of four categories of increasing degrees of unsatisfactoriness (which proved roughly equal in numbers) according to the considerations about to be described. Into Class I went those who fulfilled all of the following five criteria:

(1) They were reared by both their natural parents without any prolonged break up to the age of fifteen.
(2) Their parents preserved ordinary social standards and were not convicted criminals.
(3) The prisoners asserted that, as children, they had had a happy relationship with their parents both of whom had been good to them and shown them affection.
(4) The prisoners recalled no undue quarrelling or disharmony between their parents.
(5) None of the other evidence available contradicted the prisoners' statements on the above four points.

As many as a quarter of the prisoners fulfilled all these criteria. That is to say, in contrast to other prisoners who had had indisputably bad upbringings, these men came from unbroken homes in which social standards were reasonable and severe family discord was not outwardly apparent. This does not mean, of course, that they had all had perfectly satisfactory upbringings. One could expect to detect only the severer forms of overt disharmony by means of an enquiry so long after the event. The subtler forms of conflict situation, which may lead to delinquency, such as covert hostility disguised by parental over-solicitude, are difficult enough to bring to light with children still at home. At the time this enquiry was carried out, memories of these old conflicts would have been long since covered over by the protective rationalisations of both parents and offspring. The following examples illustrate the standards used in allocating cases to this group:

Case 67. Family Background: Class I

A divorced man of thirty-nine, whose wife had left him on account of his persistent thieving. Convicted on a total of ten occasions, his offences consisted in the main of stealing from unattended cars, but more recently he had taken to breaking into houses, and at his latest conviction nineteen such offences were taken into consideration, and the total value of goods stolen amounted to £530.

He was a small man, quietly spoken, and almost apologetic in manner. He wore a sad expression when interviewed and seemed at times on the verge of tears, although he maintained he was perfectly cheerful. Apart from some incompleteness in his version of his offences, he gave a painstaking and fairly truthful account of himself.

He was one of three children reared in a respectable, working-class setting. The family were united and stable, took part in the community activity of their local church, had many friends, and were generally well-liked. Father was always in regular employment. Although firm with his children he was also kindly and affectionate, and they were all fond of him. The mother was a good, careful provider, of placid temperament, who showed affection to all her children.

The prisoner's brother and sister both made happy marriages, and the brother achieved a position of responsibility in a local factory. The sister, who was interviewed, confirmed that their childhood was happy, and their parents united and affectionate. She said that the prisoner had been a bright, popular boy, on good terms with them all, and being the youngest he was his mother's favourite. She knew of no delinquency when he was a juvenile.

On first leaving school the prisoner worked steadily for two and a half years as an apprentice in a local firm, and then joined the forces at the age of eighteen. At this period his family regarded him as a well-behaved but quiet youth who mixed very little and never had a girl-friend. He did not like life in the forces, and several times he went sick with nervous complaints of dizziness and headache. He was first convicted at the age of twenty for burglary. He maintained that he had wandered into the house without any real intent to steal. He had been out drinking heavily with some fellow servicemen.

At the age of twenty-three, while still in the forces, he met and married a respectable girl whom he described as 'a bit hot-tempered and very determined'. Her parents felt their daughter could have made a better match, and, although they let him spend his leaves in their house, there was much tension. It was at this point in his life that he lapsed into persistent and largely irrational thieving. While on a holiday with his parents, he took a lot of articles, threw some of them away, and hoarded others. His mother thought he must have done it 'for the thrill', because he took things of no use to himself.

Shortly afterwards, he was convicted and imprisoned for a series of thefts, after which his wife's family refused to house him any longer and they separated. He then lapsed into persistent thieving, sometimes in company with others, and served two sentences of imprisonment. On his release, and to his surprise, his wife rejoined him, and for the next two and a half years he lived with her and his young son, and found and kept a steady job, and was in due course promoted to foreman. Then his wife decided that she must go back home to help nurse her mother, who had fallen ill, and she left the prisoner, taking the child with her. He felt very depressed, and almost at once started drinking and thieving again. There was a brief period of attempted reconciliation after this, and the prisoner once more went to live with his wife at her parents' home. Once again the atmosphere became tense, and after a row with his father-in-law the prisoner walked out and started stealing. He was immediately apprehended and re-imprisoned, after which his wife left him permanently. After that he was never out of prison for long. During his spells of liberty, he would find work and attend his job regularly, but in the evenings he would feel depressed and discouraged especially after repeated attempts at reconciliation with his wife failed, and would wander off on stealing forays.

In spite of his chequered history, his own parents did not reject him, and during his present imprisonment he continued a regular and affectionate correspondence with his mother, and planned to go to live with her on his release.

The above example was a man of predominantly passive-inadequate character who had never been able to overcome emotional dependency on his parents and cope with the stresses of adult life and marital responsibilities.

The next example, also from a good home, shows a totally different character. His case (58) has already been quoted (see page 68) as an illustration of extreme emotional indifference.

Case 58. Family Background: Class I

This man came from a sturdily respectable working-class home. His parents, who were interviewed, seemed a stable and devoted couple. They had lived in the same well-cared for house for thirty-nine years and had brought up eight children, all of whom, apart from the prisoner, were successfully and happily settled in life and in regular contact with their parents. The mother was a frank, unassuming person, secure in the affection of her large family, and by no means without feeling. At one point she broke into tears. She herself came from a happy home, which she described with affection. The prisoner was her first born, and she admitted to making a fuss of him. The father used to take him out and give him plenty of interest and attention.

At first, he was a good and attractive child who liked school and got on well. Following commencement at a new school at the age of eleven a remarkable change came about which the mother was at a loss to explain. He had shown no jealousy at the birth of the younger siblings and there was no change in family circumstances to account for it. He began to truant, to steal and to tell fantastic lies. When he had to go into hospital for an illness he told such stories that on visiting day the mother was confronted by an outraged nursing sister and upbraided for her supposed cruelty. It was not until he had passed forty years of age that the family as a whole began to repudiate him for his continued deceitfulness and criminality. Before that he used regularly to return home in between his prison sentences.

Cases allocated to Class II grade of family background consisted for the most part of those who had been reared in a generally affectionate, harmonious family atmosphere (i.e. fulfilling the last four of the criteria of a Class I background) but in which a separation from one or both natural parents had occurred. A few had been brought up in good foster homes, others had lost a parent by death, but in all cases apparently satisfactory and affectionate substitutes had been provided (e.g. 57, 73, 79, 82, 90, 94, 96). Also placed in this class were a few cases (e.g. 56, 77) in which independent evidence strongly suggested that the backgrounds would have been included in Class I if the prisoner had told the truth instead of pleading improbable maltreatments. A few cases (e.g. 74, 78) were put into Class II because either the parents, or their close relatives, were convicted criminals and the family could not be regarded as maintaining respectable social standards, although in respect of affection and harmoniousness the family would have qualified for Class I. In other words, Class II cases consisted of those from homes in which one feature only (most often the loss of a parent) prevented allocation to Class I.

The family backgrounds allocated to Classes III and IV consisted of those in which there was evidence that, as children, the men had been subjected to seriously disturbing influences, such as parental cruelty or rejection, quarrelsome or conflict-ridden home atmosphere, or primitive and sordid standards of care and training. Class IV included all the worst cases, those who had experienced active cruelty or extreme rejection, and those reared unhappily in harsh institutions. In Class III, homes were bad or dubious, but not without some redeeming features. In spite of unfavourable factors such as a parent missing and not replaced (e.g. 69, 71, 85), a mother who was difficult (63), repudiating (68), alcoholic (84), or deserted (81), the Class III backgrounds showed other favourable elements which seemed to have compensated to some extent. These prisoners often spoke of their childhood as having been generally happy. In some Class III cases, however (e.g. 59, 72, 95, 97), the prisoners made much of the maltreatments they had received, but social evidence suggested that their homes had not been altogether bad. The following example shows the standards used in the classification of the lower grades of family background.

Case 76. Family Background: Class IV

This was a single man aged thirty-three who fitted easily into the category of passive-inadequates. He had fifteen convictions for larceny, one for receiving and one for being found on enclosed premises. He was first convicted at the age of twelve. He had been to an approved school and to Borstal, and he had served a three-year sentence of corrective training. All his offences had been of a fortuitous, casual nature and his gains slight. The police described him as a 'persistent walk-in-thief'. On the last occasion he was sentenced for stealing five shillings from the bar of a public house during a brief absence of the landlord.

At interview he was pliant and co-operative. His mood was apathetic and depressed and he showed little resilience or vitality. Although intelligent (I.Q. 120), and conscious of his social failure, he seemed unable to understand how he had reached his present predicament, and he felt hopeless about his future. He complained that there were times when he felt extremely miserable for hours on end and would just sit on his own in a cinema with his mind rambling over his troubles. He mentioned that he had once been found wandering with 'loss of memory', and that he had a great anxiety about being forced to stay in hostels frequented by old men who might try to interfere with him sexually. He gave a truthful account of himself and he was willing for his relatives to be visited.

He was born the youngest child of a family of three children. His father worked steadily as a park attendant all his life and was a good provider, but a difficult man with a violent and unpredictable temper. His mother, a gentle, feckless, loving woman, was afraid of his father, who quarrelled with her and struck her repeatedly, on one occasion knocking her down a flight of stairs. The prisoner's brother described vividly the insecurity and fear in which they lived and the frozen terror of the household when they heard the father returning home. The prisoner was his father's favourite, and had less punishment than the others, but nevertheless he remembered how his father would come home and shout if the meal wasn't ready at once, or if he found dust on the mantelpiece. There were constant rows between his parents, and days would go by without a civil word between them. He said, 'If there was a row on pay night, Mum would have to wait for the housekeeping. Many a time she had to run out and borrow food for us.'

When the prisoner was twelve, his mother deserted with a man with whom she had been friendly for some time. She took the elder brother with her, but the prisoner and his sister, with whom he was never on very good terms, remained with the father. Soon after this he was sent away to an approved school. Thereafter, he spent most of his time in institutions. From time to time he stayed with his mother until she died, but mostly he was of 'no fixed abode', and leading a solitary, drifting, purposeless existence. He never had a girl-friend. His connections with his relatives were tenuous and lukewarm. He never stayed in a job for long.

Table 28 shows the results of various comparisons between prisoners from the four grades of family background. The fact that a half of them came from manifestly unsatisfactory homes (Classes III or IV) confirmed the association of criminality and disordered upbringing which previous investigators have noted with depressing regularity. At the same time, the fact that a quarter came from homes that were to outward appearance satisfactory showed that the association was not so invariable as it generally supposed.

Since disordered homes have been held responsible for the development of both criminality and personality deviation, one would have expected that the most damaged personalities, namely the extreme inadequates, to have originated from the worst homes. No such trend appeared. Neither passive-inadequacy nor psychopathic emotional indifferences occurred significantly more often or more prominently among those from bad homes. If anything, the worst homes yielded the fewest instances of serious emotional indifference. Furthermore, some of the most extreme deviants (e.g. Case 58, page 87) were products of the better homes, and the few non-deviant personalities came from all types of backgrounds.

Considering the complexity of the situation it is perhaps not so surprising that a crude grading of manifest family disturbance failed to correlate with subsequent personality disorder. However, one fairly direct relationship for which some evidence did appear was between experience of active cruelty or violence in childhood and subsequent aggressiveness of personality. Three of the preventive detainees were thought to have undergone seriously violent treatment as children. The only example of severe impulsive aggressiveness (score 2) among the preventive detainees was one of these three. Of three intermittent recidivists who had also experienced violence in childhood, two were among the small group of eight prisoners in whom the trait of impulsive aggression was pronounced.

2. Relative Normality of those from Criminal Backgrounds

The absence of a straightforward relationship between family background and personality deviation led to an attempt to explore further the interplay between family influences and individual reactions. For this purpose the prisoners' histories were compared with those of their siblings, especially their brothers. This was done for the preventive detainees only because the necessary information was less often available in the case of the intermittent recidivists.

As already explained, most of the prisoners were the only offenders in their families. The minority who had criminal relatives seemed on the whole to be less deviant in personality than most of the prisoners. Nine preventive detainees had a brother or half-brother known to have had a criminal conviction. These nine, although they mostly came from the worst backgrounds (five from Class IV and only one, Case 88, from Class I) showed relatively little neurotic tendency and relatively few psychopathic traits.[1] In spite of this their backgrounds were at least as bad, if not worse, than the general run of prisoners. If they had not lacked parental affection, then they had lacked many other things. For example, Case 78 (Class II) came from a poverty-stricken home in a delinquent neighbourhood. He said: 'The other fellows were stealing. I got into it with them.' In Case 74 (Class II) the parents were as affectionate as could be desired, but their standards in other directions were lamentable. Both parents had had criminal convictions and they were known to encourage their children to

[1] Only one rated 2 and five rated 0 on neurotic tendency. On the neuroticism scale of the M.P.I., only one had a really high score, exceeded by 12 per cent of those tested. On emotional indifference six had the lowest ratings (0 or 1) and none had the highest ratings (5 or 6).

steal. It would seem that, from the psychological standpoint, if more than one member of the family takes to crime this is a good sign, perhaps because it reflects adverse social pressures rather than individual weakness.

3. The 'Black-Sheep' Phenomenon

In marked contrast to the nine with criminal brothers, another nine preventive detainees were the conspicuous 'black-sheep' of good (Class I) families. The brothers of these nine were not just non-criminal, they were responsible, stable persons and usually the fathers of happy families. The 'black-sheep' themselves, however, were not merely criminal, they were also conspicuously abnormal. Apart from the two fairly ordinary men (60, 62) whose criminal habits only became prominent after they had contracted unhappy marriages, all the others were seriously disturbed or severely deviant. They included several of the worst neurotics. One was a psychotic with a history of epilepsy and serious nervous disorder in childhood (Case 51, page 109). One was a pathological liar with very marked psychopathic indifference (Case 58, pages 68 and 87). One was a hypochondrical neurotic who had been invalided from the forces with neuraesthenia (66). Another who had also had nervous illnesses while in the forces was an excessively inadequate neurotic (67). Two were mentally dull. One had an I.Q. of 79 and a plethora of nervous symptoms dating from a severe head injury in childhood (92), which left him with permanent facial palsy and subject to headaches and bad moods. The other dullard was a typically apathetic, socially isolated, feckless inadequate (99). Finally, one was an intelligent but odd person who suffered from psychogenic skin disorder and had shown pronounced neurotic traits in childhood (75). In all of these abnormals the behaviour disturbance had begun in childhood. Since these conspicuous 'black-sheep' present something of a challenge to psychological interpretations, two examples not previously quoted are given below:

Case 99

A single man, fifty years old, with ten convictions for breaking and entering or larceny, and one for indecent assault on a female. This was his first court appearance, and occurred when he was nineteen. He said he had had no previous experience of women and had been 'dared' into it by a fellow at work. He was below average in intelligence (I.Q. 87).

He was brought up in a respectable, industrious family who lived for many years in the same house in a small country-town. His mother cared well for all her eight children. He was the eldest son and particularly devoted to her, although he said, he was not her favourite.

His early life was uneventful, and he was not a bad worker, although dull and dependent. He fell into tempers if he could not get his own way at home, and he was inclined to bully his younger siblings. His brothers, who were all more intelligent and ambitious, felt him a liability. One of them described him as 'the odd one out' and remarked, 'I knew he would never get a woman to look after him and that he would always be at home.' As he grew older he became more and more rejected by the family, and only his mother protected him. After her death, when he was twenty-eight, his thieving increased in frequency, and in the past twelve years he had spent only nine months outside prison. On the last occasion, he surrendered to the police. 'It was cold and I had no money,' he said. 'Either I had to get some more or give myself up.' Once before under similar circumstances he had done the same. 'Otherwise I could have gone from bad to worse. But I didn't expect P.D. But I can't grumble, I've had seven chances and they warned me.'

The prisoner was conscious of his own failure in life. 'I suppose I was headstrong, I wanted my own way.' He said that at night he lay awake thinking of the years he had wasted and of how his mother would have grieved. 'I do feel I've been wicked breaking into other people's houses. Maybe those people have been saving that money for weeks. Maybe they're worse off than I am.' He had no plans for his discharge and he was well aware that he could expect no help from his relatives.

Case 75

A married man aged forty-one with three children, he was one of the few preventive detainees who was actually living with his wife at the time of his latest conviction. He had a record of ten convictions for offences of stealing and for breaking in. He made a speciality of stealing from churches and large country houses, and he was very persistent in his habits, admitting to 162 offences on the occasion of his latest conviction.

He was an intelligent man (I.Q. 118) who seemed always to have been preoccupied with theological and political concepts. At one time he had wanted to become a Roman Catholic priest. During his present imprisonment he wrote to the Unitarian Church Council and had one of their ministers visit him. The minister was surprised at the extent of his knowledge, and at his apparent contentment with reading and studying in prison. After his interviews with the psychiatrist, he wrote a long, neatly written letter asking an opinion about existentialism and about paranormal phenomena.

He mentioned that he had first started breaking-in as a boy of twelve when he was paid by some pro-Communist members of the International Labour Party to enter cotton mills and slash the material on the looms. His interests appear to have changed later, for a police report recorded the presence of tattoo marks in the form of a swastika and the words 'British Legion of Fascists'.

He was the elder and favourite son of doting, ambitious parents. He gave an idyllic version of their kindness and perfect parental behaviour. They were visited, and their devotion to the prisoner, whom they constantly referred to as 'our John', was abundantly obvious, but they gave the impression of being over-possessive and dominating, in spite of their good intentions. They were apt to blame the prisoner's wife and her spendthrift habits for his thieving, although the habit was established long before he married her. The parents had both risen from humble origins, but now they took an active part in community activities and adopted considerable social pretensions.

As a child the prisoner was over-inhibited, clever, well-behaved, obedient, and excessively devoted to his mother. He did not mix well with other children and preferred reading at home. In addition, he was reserved and unconfiding, a trait also noticed, and complained of, by his wife and by the Unitarian minister.

The prisoner maintained that his early adolescent offences were committed out of sheer devilment. He entered the army as a boy recruit, and the offences ceased for a time, but began again when he was discharged on account of an ear infection. He was thereupon committed to Borstal. On release he soon got married, but his offences began again and continued when he was re-called to the forces, from which he was prematurely discharged following a further conviction. He blamed his wife's extravagance and debts for the prolongation of his criminal career, saying that she nagged him into thieving for her. The wife maintained that she had no idea he was still thieving, since he left home as if to go to work and always arrived back at the expected times. Her story could hardly have been true, since the police reported that the offences took place in the hours of darkness.

In spite of this source of dispute, the prisoner and his wife got along together well in other ways, and brought up a family of three children successfully. They never thought of parting, although his parents had urged him to do so. He had no difficulty finding jobs or keeping them until such time as he was caught thieving.

The wife mentioned that he was very quiet, not one for making friends, and very secretive. She felt she never knew what he was doing, or thinking. She thought he was too much dominated by his mother, but he was very affectionate to herself and the children. He had always suffered from skin trouble of nervous origin. A specialist opinion obtained during his present imprisonment read: 'The lesions on the hands and face are self-inflicted and come under the heading of dermatitis autophytica.'

At interview he expressed some feelings of guilt. 'It bothers me when I think about it. I've sinned against society and God himself.' He readily explained to the psychiatrist, as he had also told the police, that he had been engaged in thieving during the whole of his last three-year period of liberty. 'I like to get things cleared,' he remarked, 'I've always told the police.'

He agreed he did not like to mix with workmates. 'They have bad habits I don't like.' Also, and for the same reason, he has never mixed with thieves since he was a boy.

The contrast between the relative normality of the prisoners from criminal broods and the abnormality of the 'black-sheep' of good families suggests that personality deviation and criminal habits, though they frequently coincide in the same individual, may have different origins. It may be that the more obvious types of family disturbance, broken homes, parental quarrels or neglect, and extraneous influence such as financial depression and delinquent companions, engender criminal habits, often in more than one of their offspring, but do not necessarily cause substantial damage to personality. Indeed, in such situations, by providing some outlet for frustrated emotions, the criminal acts might serve as a safeguard against psychological disturbance. On the other hand, the kind of criminality which results from severe personality disorder may arise quite differently, especially if the factors responsible operate so as to single out one member of an otherwise stable family. In such cases, the important factors might be less closely connected with faulty upbringing. For example, an innate psycho-physical defect, due to brain injury or disease, may affect only one member of an otherwise normal family and create difficulties for him in social adjustment. This sort of explanation would account rather plausibly for several of the 'black-sheep', two of whom were dullards and two of whom had suffered definite brain injury or disease in childhood. However in many cases it is unnecessary to fall back upon explanations in terms of hypothetical constitutional weakness. Evidently some outwardly satisfactory homes may harbour concealed and damaging psychological influences directed against one member of the family. In the last example quoted (75), the tensely over-ambitious parents clearly favoured their intelligent and enterprising criminal son over his law-abiding but duller brother. Although unaware of doing so, they probably encouraged him and obtained some vicarious satisfaction from his crimes. In most instances, however, the interplay between individual temperament and family behaviour is probably more important than either factor in isolation. In Case 99, for example, the prisoner would not have been rejected and left to fend for himself had he not been so far behind his siblings in intelligence and energy.

Another possible explanation of the 'black-sheep' phenomenon is that transient disturbances in an otherwise stable family (such as the temporary absence of mother through illness) if they occur at a critical time in the emotional development of one of the children, may affect him badly while leaving his siblings unscathed. No positive evidence for this appeared in the data collected in this investigation, but the histories of the prisoners' infancy obtained from relatives was hardly sufficient to assess this factor properly.

4. Age of Onset of Crime

There was also an association between family background and age at onset of crime, in that those from apparently good (Class I) homes tended to have no penal record as juveniles and to have their first criminal conviction in their twenties (see Table 28). In general, the worse the home background the earlier the onset of crime. This result confirmed Taylor's findings on preventive detainees (see p. 18) which indicated an association between conflict-ridden home backgrounds and relatively early onset of crime. This relationship, which is clearly a most important one, suggests that a satisfactory home background, although providing a shield against juvenile delinquency, may have less relevance in the case of the late-comer to crime.

An examination of the circumstances of onset of criminal habits yielded some more information on this point. None of the prisoners admitted to a deliberate choice of crime as a career. Most of them blamed difficult or trying circumstances, and in the case of the late-comers to crime the difficulties most often cited were those attendant upon leaving home and undertaking adult responsibilities for the first time. In eighteen of the fifty preventive detainees, loss of the support provided by the parental home seemed to be a prominent factor concerned with the onset of criminal habits. Most of these men came from the better home backgrounds (eight from Class I, five from II and only five from either III or IV). Here is a typical example:

Case 86

A divorced man, aged forty-three, with a record of nine convictions each one including charges of fraud or false pretences, mostly arising from passing dud cheques.

He was the only boy of very affectionate, united and respectable parents who somewhat over-protected and indulged him as a child (Class I background). He described his father as 'one of the best you could wish for' and his mother as 'worth her weight in gold'. He said she 'gave us everything we wanted' and 'never punished us'. A home visit to the mother confirmed the substance of this account. He had no court appearances as a juvenile, and the only early delinquency his mother could recall was a brief episode of stealing fruit and such-like at the age of eleven. As a child, he was most affectionate and attentive to his mother.

He left home to marry at the age of twenty-two, and very soon after, at the beginning of 39–45 war, he joined the forces and was posted abroad. He did not like it, he said, because he didn't seem to mix with his fellow servicemen. He started drinking heavily and misapplying funds entrusted to him. After imprisonment and discharge with ignominy he returned to his wife. His mother noticed that he was changed. He had become a reckless spendthrift and boaster. He took to sending expensive presents to his parents without paying for them, and he was continually giving dud cheques to tradesmen. His father spent some £500 in an effort to cover his misdeeds, but eventually he swindled an employer of £1,000 and was convicted and imprisoned.

His wife stayed with him for ten years. He was gentle and affectionate in his sexual behaviour and, she says, 'I could not believe each time that he could behave so badly. I forgave him over and over again.' They lived together in various rooms and hotels, but he was for ever piling up debts and then disappearing, leaving her to placate landladies and creditors. She finally divorced him on account of repeated infidelities with other women, to whom he posed as a bachelor.

At his first interview with the psychiatrist he was inclined to adopt the air of a martyr, and to produce elaborate explanations by way of extenuating his offences. At a second interview he was more shamefaced and quieter spoken. He expressed vague ideas of inferiority. 'I often feel that everyone is looking at me and I think they know about my past.' 'I've always had that feeling. Some sort of myth against me. People at work seem to put upon me.' He gave this symptom as a reason for his customary sequence of behaviour, first getting tense and upset about it, then going out and drinking heavily, and ending up on a thieving and sexual spree lasting until the inevitable arrest.

Like Case 67, quoted on page 86, the above example shows a man who first broke down on leaving a protective parental home. Unlike the previous example, this man was classed as an active rather than a passive deviant. His superficial sociability, his sexual adventures, his enjoyment of the spoils of crime and his enterprise and aplomb in carrying off daring deceptions all fitted in with the actively predatory attitude, accompanied by a high degree of emotional indifference. It is of some interest, however, that on being confronted at the second interview by a sympathetic but firm resumé of the true course of his life, he switched to anxious, self-critical attitudes and ideas of inferiority more typical of the neurotic inadequate. Such a metamorphosis suggests that in some cases outward psychopathic indifference conceals inner insecurity and sense of inadequacy. This may, perhaps, account for the overlap between neurotic and psychopathic features evident in many cases.

In most of the late-comers to crime who first lapsed after leaving the parental home, various contributing factors added to the stress experienced at that time. Sometimes the break coincided with the onset of family troubles in a previously harmonious environment. In Case 99 for example (see page 92) the prisoner was still living at home at the age of twenty-three when quarrels flared up unexpectedly and his parents separated. He went to stay with an aunt, made the acquaintance of some delinquent drinking companions, and started thieving for the first time. In another case (100) the prisoner's mother left home at the outbreak of war to go to stay with a sister in the country. His father took a mistress in her absence and bribed him not to tell. 'He gave me a lot of money so I just lay about without working.' At the same time he began to drink heavily, which called for still more money, so he and a friend tried to steal a typewriter, and this led to his first conviction at the age of eighteen. He then went into the forces, did not like it, deserted and lived by theft until caught and imprisoned.

Some of the men from the less favourable backgrounds avoided conviction until some further deterioration in their family circumstances left them entirely on their own. For example, in two cases (54, 81) quarrels with relatives took place when the men returned from service in the forces, and this led to them setting out on their own to make their way by thieving. Another man (59) left his parental home at the age of twenty-five because his father had died and he no longer felt welcome. Immediately he took to heavy drinking and consequent stealing.

It seems clear that the stage of breaking away from the parental home proved a critical testing time for many prisoners, especially for those who had enjoyed the protection of a stable home. In such cases the age of onset of crime may be quite advanced. Of the preventive detainees who had been substantially honest while living at home, all but two reached the twenties or thirties before their first conviction.

In a recent study of inmates of a Canadian penitentiary Cormier[1] reported that among those who started criminal habits relatively late in life and then went on to become recidivists certain types predominated. Prominent among them was the inadequate, the sort of man who, despite normal intelligence, found a generalised difficulty in coping with life. Such persons were safe so long as they remained within a protective family circle, but when they came of an age to compete at work and in the world at large they resorted to crime. Cormier also found that neurotics were particularly common among late-coming recidivists. These were men who had shown prominent neurotic tendencies in childhood and had only later begun to 'act out' the conflicts and discontents that they had previously expressed in the form of symptoms.

Up to a point the present findings agreed with those reported by Cormier. Most of the late-comers were classed as inadequates, and some two-thirds of them complained of neurotic symptoms. Since these late-comers mostly originated in the better homes, this constituted further evidence that personality deviants, especially inadequates, can be shielded from crime so long as they are kept in a suitably sheltered and undemanding environment. However, since a substantial proportion of those from bad homes who began their crimes early were also inadequates, this feature could not be said to characterise late-coming recidivists more than recidivists generally.

[1] Cormier, B. *et al.*, 'The Problem of Recidivism and the Treatment of the Late-comer to Crime', *Canadian Journ. Corrections*, 1961, 3, 51–65.

X

CONCLUDING REFLECTIONS

ALTHOUGH some obvious trends emerged from this survey, it is equally apparent, as others have observed before,[1] that habitual prisoners include many different types, and that no generalisations will cover all cases. Some are skilful criminals, others petty sneak-thieves, some are heartily symptom free, others severely neurotic or frankly mad, some are fathers of stable families, others hopeless drifters and social isolates, some are the products of loveless, deprived homes and some have had good parents. Interest lies in the relative frequency of these various features compared with what is expected or found among offenders in general.

Contrary to the popular stereotype of a persistent criminal, few of these prisoners were prone to violence and hardly any were efficiently organized, professional criminals. The majority were shiftless, work-shy characters for whom petty stealing represented the line of least resistance. The high proportion of housebreakers, unusual for men of mature years, reflected the persistence of crude methods of thieving learned in youth rather than the acquirement of special skill in burglary. The incidence of psychiatric symptoms was much higher than anticipated. Ten per cent were or had been psychotic and a further sixteen per cent had been admitted to hospital or discharged from the forces on psychiatric grounds. Altogether, at least a third had a history of severe mental disorder. It seemed likely that the higher incidence of psychosis among preventive detainees was due to the fact that they had been under observation consistently over a long period. The presence of so many mentally disturbed individuals is a strong argument in favour of careful psychiatric screening of habitual offenders. When the Observation Centres for adults come fully into operation, it may be possible to have a psychiatric assessment and report on all cases with a history of more than (say) six convictions on indictment. Certainly all those under consideration for preventive

[1] See for instance: *Report of the Departmental Committee on Persistent Offenders*, Cmd. 4090, London, 1932.

detention warrant more than the brief formal statement that is usually submitted to the Court. For instance, among the fifty cases examined, it is unlikely that a second period of preventive detention would have been given to a deteriorating paranoid schizophrenic (95) or that the schizoid man who stole knickers from a clothes line and was later certified (51) would have gone to preventive detention at all, had the results of a full psychological investigation been available to the Courts.

Apart from actual symptoms, the great majority of the prisoners (eighty-eight per cent) were severely deviant in personality, and apparently unable to respond normally to other people or to function adequately in the roles expected of responsible adults. In some cases, this was because their peculiarly egocentric and predatory attitudes rendered all their relationships superficial and short-lived, but more often it was on account of excessively withdrawn, solitary habits coupled with neurotic complaints and morbid sensitivity. In effect, these prisoners were much more often like chronic neurotics of inadequate personality than the conventional picture of aggressive psychopathic delinquents. The fact that at an average age of forty, a half of the preventive detainees had never been married and only eight per cent were living with wives provided a good measure of the extent of their social disturbance. Many were excessive drinkers or gamblers. Sexual relationships tended to be conspicuously lacking or else fleeting and promiscuous, and perversions were common.

Classification by type of personality deviation served to distinguish groups of prisoners presenting contrasting problems of management and treatment. The following categories were used:

I. *The Non-Deviants* (Twelve per cent)

These have no formal mental illness, no serious neurosis, and their personality is not such as to prevent them from getting along among their chosen group of friends, or of enjoying satisfactory marital and family relationships. They constitute the so-called 'socialised delinquents' who are well adjucted to a criminal milieu. Such men tend towards the professional type of crime specialising in relatively ambitious offences aimed at property of considerable value. They organise and plan their criminal activities rationally, they co-operate with others in carrying them through, and they may succeed many times before being finally apprehended. Although lacking in respect for other people's property, they experience the normal restraints of conscience in their personal life, and are unlikely to commit atrocious or irrationally violent offences against individuals.

II. *Active-Aggressive Deviants* (Thirty-six per cent)

These men are actively predatory in their attitudes and habits and tend to show to a marked degree the psychopathic qualities of 'emotional indifference'. Only a minority, however, are physically violent or explosively aggressive. Although superficially outgoing and sociable, their relationships are shallow and short lived, for fundamentally they regard their fellow men with hostility and suspicion. They pursue their goals heedless of consequences of others, and their offences take the form of deliberate, active attacks on the law-abiding community. Habitual deceivers and confidence tricksters and pathological liars most often belong to this group, as do the more daring and dangerous offenders. When their deviance is extreme, and especially if they are prone to impulsive violence, their condition approximates to the classic descriptions of the criminal psychopath.

III. *Passive Inadequate Deviants* (Fifty-two per cent)

This is the largest group among habitual prisoners. They consist of ineffective, feckless people, conspicuously lacking in drive, many of them excessively solitary and friendless, but prone to dependency and parasitism when they get the chance. They generally go in for thieving on a petty scale, usually committed alone and on impulse when, as happens all too often, they find themselves faced with difficulties.

Although few of the men classed in this group were strictly speaking sub-normal, their average intelligence was lower than the other groups, and they included a considerably higher proportion of individuals with psychiatric symptoms. They also included most of those who had been convicted of deviant sex behaviour (homosexuality, molestation of children and exhibitionism). On psychological testing, as well as by clinical observation, they were on average less extraverted and more neurotic than the active-aggressive deviants. They also showed less of the psychopathic traits of emotional indifference. There was, however, a considerable overlap, in so far as a substantial number of prisoners had both psychopathic and neurotic traits simultaneously.

Although evolved independently, the division into active-aggressive and passive inadequate types follows closely the classification suggested by Marcus, except that he envisaged a continuous variation, with extreme examples at opposite poles, and most cases in between. In fact, there is probably no real dichotomy, but for the purpose of deciding appropriate treatment or disposal, allocation to one side or the other according to the

> dominant trends has practical advantages. Since a few well defined features (e.g. type and scope of crime, scores on the M.P.I. questionnaire, presence of complaints or symptoms) all correlate substantially with the aggressivity — passivity assessment, classification could be based upon a simple routine procedure without resort to psychiatric interviews. Marcus included all prisoners in his analysis, but here the small number of non-deviants were left in a class of their own. In their general attitude and type of crime the non-deviants resembled active aggressives much more than passive-inadequates.

Exploration of family background and early upbringing, within the limits of the material available, yielded findings that warrant further investigation. Enough of the prisoners came from apparently good homes to allow for comparisons with those from the deprived and disordered homes. Those from the worst homes more often started their criminal careers as juveniles. Those with criminal siblings (a fair indication of environmental pressures) were on the whole the least peculiar psychologically. The solitary 'black sheep' of seemingly good families included some of the most seriously pathological cases whose peculiarities had been outstandingly obvious from their earliest years. There was no demonstrable connection between type of home background and type of adult personality deviation. These findings suggest that the relationship between disordered home circumstances and later criminality is more complex than generally supposed. It may be that different sets of factors lead by different routes to the end result of crime. Neglectful, disorganised homes in bad neighbourhoods produce rebellion and delinquency in relatively normal children. Factors which cause personality damage or mental illness may lead to crime in later life by rendering the individual unfit to fend for himself without parental protection.

The outcome of this survey contrasts sharply with findings reported elsewhere in connection with persistent criminals. For instance, in a study of men sentenced to protective custody in Finland, A. Ahto[1] found that they rarely came from respectable families (eighty-one per cent of homes were classed as 'wretched' and 96·32 as 'neglectful'; 29·7 per cent of fathers and 47·1 per cent of brothers were ex-convicts, and a half of the parents were classed as psychopaths), that their first convictions usually occurred at an early age (86·5 per cent under twenty-one), that a substantial

[1] Ahto, A., *Dangerous Habitual Criminals*, Helsinki, 1951.

proportion committed offences of serious violence, and that two-fifths were mentally dull or severely subnormal. In order to qualify for protective custody under Finnish law a man must be a 'dangerous' criminal as well as an 'habitual' criminal, and he must have committed a serious new crime punishable by a minimum penalty of three years of penal servitude. The differences are therefore most likely due to selection. In England men may go into preventive detention for small-scale offences, provided they commit them often enough, so that the inmates of our detention centres, like the inmates of prisons for recidivists, consist predominantly of feckless characters who rarely succeed in maintaining themselves for long outside of prison. A man with a large number of convictions, and repeated sentences of imprisonment is therefore much more likely to be a psychiatric case or a hopeless inadequate than a dangerously violent gangster or a well organised bank robber. Those who commit the most serious crimes of all (e.g. murderers, rapists) are essentially non-repeaters. Those professional crooks whose operations constitute the most serious menace to valuable property are most likely to be found outside of prison. The conclusion is not that the malignant psychopath or the dangerously violent criminal does not exist, but that he is rarely found among the sort of men who are in and out of prison all their lives and finally end in preventive detention.

Suggestions as to Treatment

The inadequate group is the most important, both as regards numbers and as regards the possibility of providing effective help. The study of conviction-free intervals showed that at least some of the inadequates were capable of giving up criminal habits for long periods of time, and even doing a reasonable job of work so long as they remained in sheltered circumstances and under the personal protection of someone prepared to look after them and make allowances for their shortcomings. This conclusion is confirmed by the experience of Merfyn Turner, who started the Norman House Hostels for former prisoners. He found that inadequates did better than other types under the kindly, supportive, family atmosphere he and his wife provided.

His definition of inadequates corresponded closely with that used in this report. He writes:[1]

[1] Turner, M., *Norman House: The First Five Years*, London, privately printed, 1961. See also: Turner, M., *Safe Lodging*, London, 1961.

> 'The inadequates appeared to have arrived at their position as a result of repeated social failure. They had failed at school, at work, and in some cases in the forces. Most of them were unmarried. They had no friends who could help to support them. They drifted into their crime. In prison, they promised themselves there could be no next time. They were too ill-equipped to prevent it.'

In the Norman House setting the inadequates found themselves sympathetically accepted and tolerated and were stimulated to try to respond accordingly. This meant they had to learn to stay in their jobs and to curb their habit of wandering away whenever any strain or difficulty presented itself. Some learned sufficiently well to carry on unaided after discharge. Many of them, however, relapsed almost immediately they left the protection of the hostel, but hardly any did so while still living in Norman House. The result of Merfyn Turner's social experiment supports the contention of this report that inadequates are not necessarily criminals from choice and that many of them may give up crime so long as they find emotional acceptance and a measure of protection against a world that seems to them too harshly demanding.

Turner was less optimistic about those in whom inadequacy was complicated by specific psychiatric problems, such as sexual disorder, alcohol addiction, prominent neurotic problems or psychotic tendency. He felt that for such persons the hostel provided a temporary refuge but left them to face the world again with the same difficulties as before. He was probably right. We do not know what proportion of cases will respond sufficiently to become independent, or how long such a result may take. Hostels for inadequates need to be organised like establishments for the mentally abnormal, on the assumption that support will carry on indefinitely, or for however long the individual cannot fend for himself without it. The essential feature about such hostels is that they should be on a small scale, with a maximum of personal attention, so as to establish a family atmosphere and enable the inmates to form a stable, dependent relationship.

Not all the offenders in the inadequate group could be dealt with by placement in a motherly hostel. Those who have broken down into major mental illness — psychotic depression or paranoid schizophrenia — require hospitalisation and drugs as much as any other patient with a similar illness. It is plausible to suppose, however, that in some cases these more serious breakdowns might be avoided or postponed if the inadequate's particular needs could be met at an earlier stage.

To accomplish this treatment regime the inadequates have first to be identified, and this calls for leisurely and thorough psychological examinations, such as the preventive detainees received at the Wandsworth allocation centre. It is important that examinations should include interviews with relatives, both for the purpose of assessing the social background and for checking the veracity of the prisoner's version of himself. The ideal time for this would be during remand, so that the Courts could have the benefit of the results before passing sentence.

If appropriate hostels were available, it would be possible to make residence in them a condition of probation, and that might provide a convenient alternative to prison for many inadequates. Alternatively, there is no reason in principle why suitable candidates among those already in preventive detention should not be allocated at an early stage of their sentence to hostels within the prison service. This would effectively convert preventive detention from a depressingly custodial regime to a long period of social training under sheltered conditions. It would open the door to meaningful decisions about remission of sentence or release on licence based upon the trustworthiness or otherwise of the offender's performance in the community. Under the present system, compliant response to the minimal demands of a closed institution, which bears little relation to the likelihood of adjustment outside, weighs too heavily in decisions about remission. A prison hostel system of the type suggested here would call for a sophisticated selection of cases, so as deliberately to avoid the intelligent, outstanding fast-talkers and favour the more repugnant, whining inadequates.

As things are, too many inadequates find their way to high-security prisons, where they languish for years at high cost to the state, and become increasingly institutionalised and increasingly dependent. Although a great nuisance, they hardly constitute a dangerous menace. Public concern about such prisoners escaping is exaggerated. Attention might be directed more profitably to the much greater number of undetected thieves at large in the community. If a hostel regime suffices to keep inadequates under control on probation, and encourages them to try to make their way in honest work, this would seem a better solution for all concerned. The risk that when the limited period of their probation orders expire these offenders would leave their hostels and recommence thieving might be less than anticipated. Experience suggests that inadequates readily become dependent upon help provided, and once their dependency is well established they become reluctant to leave.

Even without benefit of a hostel, it might be that a devoted probation officer could place some of these inadequates in the right kind of lodgings and give them sufficient attention and support to keep them out of prison for long periods. Among the preventive detainees of this survey only thirty-six per cent had ever had a period on probation. (In Hammond's survey the figure was thirty-five per cent.)

Some judicial authorities may have come already to the conclusion that preventive detention is inappropriate to the inadequate type of offender. At the Court of Criminal Appeal on 19 May 1961, a sentence of three years' probation was substituted for one of twelve years' preventive detention. Mr Justice Pilcher was reported as saying to the offender: 'Despite your record you are not a violent man. Your trouble is that you are a completely ineffective man. You don't seem to be able even to commit a crime properly.'[1]

On 26 February 1962, the Lord Chief Justice, Lord Parker, at a sitting of the Court of Criminal Appeal, said that too much use was being made of the power to impose preventive detention in the case of prisoners of thirty to thirty-five years of age, and that in over thirty per cent of appeals such sentences were varied to periods of imprisonment. He warned that after preventive detention a prisoner is liable to become institutionalised, and that therefore it should only be given as a last resort. He pointed out that in the case of serious crime a sentence of imprisonment of sufficient length to give adequate protection to the public may often properly be given.[2]

The management of the active aggressive personality deviants presents a much tougher problem and no ready-made or administratively simple solutions are apparent. In so far as these types are more resourceful than the inadequates, their potentiality for change should be greater. Unfortunately, though expediency often compels them to regret their crimes and to adopt a superficially respectful pose, they lack feeling for the harm they do to others, and their underlying attitude to authority is actively hostile and

[1] The *Guardian*, 20 May 1961. [2] *Criminal Appeal Reports*, 1962, 46, 234.

resistant. They are less likely than the inadequates to co-operate voluntarily in any reformative or therapeutic scheme, and so provision for them has to be planned within a prison setting. They respond poorly to individual psychotherapy on conventional lines, possibly because they are predominantly extraverted characters, and have little interest in analysing their own motives. A regime appropriate to such characters has been evolved at the Henderson Hospital. It makes use of frequent group discussions combined with a community organisation exerting heavy social pressure towards mutual co-operation and constructive occupation. Listening to the recital of other people's annoyances and frustrations, and forced to come to terms with others of similar egocentric, insincere and predatory attitudes, the offender finds himself reluctantly impelled to face up to some of his own shortcomings. Experience at such centres as Herstedvester in Denmark and the Van den Hoeven Clinic at Utrecht, shows that a concerted psychiatric attack will make an impression on a proportion of actively hostile criminals. The protective crust of emotional indifference can break down, and the erstwhile psychopath becomes an anxious, treatable neurotic. Unfortunately, the organisation of such a complex and expensive therapeutic regime within our over-crowded prisons, and the provision for its continuance according to individual needs regardless of length of sentence, seems altogether impractical with facilities at present available. Nevertheless, the ideal is perhaps worth mentioning if only to draw attention to the wide gap between theoretical indications and practical possibilities in England.

Appendix I

FURTHER EXAMPLES OF PSYCHOSIS AMONG PREVENTIVE DETAINEES

Case 51

This man was sentenced to seven years' preventive detention at the age of thirty-five following a conviction for stealing from a clothes line a pair of gloves and ladies' nylon underwear. No other offences were taken into consideration on that occasion, which was his tenth conviction.

He had always been regarded as a solitary and peculiar individual. As a child he suffered from frequent epileptic fits, thought to have followed an attack of measles in infancy. He was timid and bullied by other children, and has obsessional habits of incessantly washing his hands and polishing his shoes. He was excessively attached to his mother, who was herself very hypochondrical.

In his teens he stayed, on different occasions, a total of seventeen months in an epileptic colony. When he passed through the allocation centre the year following his conviction he was thought by the psychologist to be an incipient psychotic. For several months already he had been complaining about other prisoners spreading tales against him. Three months after his transfer to a central prison he was admitted to the hospital one night shouting excitedly in response to hallucinatory voices. He complained of sensations caused by people getting inside his body. Under treatment with the drug 'stelazine', he became quieter and lost some of his delusions. He was seen at an outside mental hospital sixteen months later. He was still under drug treatment, in spite of which he gave a muddled account of vaguely persecutory and sexual preoccupations, interspersed with hypochondrical delusions, all of which he described with the fatuous cheerfulness typical of schizophrenics.

Case 83

When seen at the allocation centre this prisoner was noted by the psychologist to be a rather withdrawn person, who related wild fantasies about being engaged on research in colour television. There was evidence of mental deterioration in the results of intelligence testing. (Verbal I.Q. 90, performance I.Q. 72, full-scale I.Q. 81 on the *Wechsler Adult Intelligence Scale.*) Three months after transfer to a central prison, he began complaining of hearing voices and seemed confused.

He improved temporarily on the drug chlorpromazine, but relapsed a year later, becoming heedless of appearance and cleanliness, and intensely preoccupied with delusions and hallucinations about interference by radar machines from outer space. He improved, but only temporarily, following transfer to a mental hospital. He was still talking about being molested by radar waves when he disappeared from the hospital and from all possibility of further investigations.

Case 87

At the age of twenty-two, having been convicted on six occasions for sexual and/or thieving offences, this man was certified as a moral defective and remained in institutions for criminal lunatics for six and a half years, until he escaped and changed his name. He subsequently obtained various posts as a schoolmaster, which usually terminated by dismissal or conviction for sexual misbehaviour with the boys.

He was still single, and aged forty-eight, when sentenced to preventive detention following conviction for buggery with a boy of fifteen. He had in fact complained of 'voices' for some five years, but some authorities were inclined to suspect malingering. Apart from being notably solitary and withdrawn, he had been able to support himself outside prison and stay with friends without their in the least suspecting mental illness. Notes were available of an interview by an outside psychiatrist shortly after his last arrest. The opinion given was: 'There seems little doubt that this man is a paranoid schizophrenic (showing mannerisms, perplexity, auditory and somatic hallucinations, and thought blocking).' When the prisoner passed through the allocation centre a year later the psychologist noted that the intelligence test results indicated a man, formerly of superior intelligence, but now considerably deteriorated owing to his psychopathological state. (Verbal I.Q. 122, performance 109, full-scale 117, *Wechsler Adult Intelligence Scale.*)

At interview four years after his conviction he presented a clear picture of chronic paranoid schizophrenia in a quiescent phase. His emotional responses seemed blunted and inappropriate. He showed no concern over his physical condition, although he was in hospital with angina pectoris, and there was no change in his flat, whining tone of voice when he discussed his sexual perversion. He prattled in a vague, disjointed fashion about irrelevancies, and kept making childish allusions to having been rejected by his mother. He admitted to hearing voices still, but maintained that they were not so bad now. He could not be prevailed upon to explain what they said, apart from calling his name and interfering with his thoughts. He showed signs of perplexity of thought, frequently referring in a puzzled way to what he called 'The coincidence', which he seemed unable to explain.

Case 91

This was a single man, sentenced to preventive detention at the age of thirty-nine after conviction for stealing a mirror and some keys from a car. The Court asked for a supplementary medical examination. The prisoner complained of pain and weakness in his shoulders which he attributed to extractions of teeth by a prison dentist. He said he had committed the offence to call attention to his grievances. The medical officer considered him 'a paranoid psychopath' but 'not certifiable'.

During his period of detention his persecutory ideas increased, and he created disturbances by breaking up his cell and fighting. He was transferred to a prison hospital and diagnosed as a paranoid schizophrenic with bizarre persecutory delusions. On heavy doses of chlorpromazine he became less agitated, but remained preoccupied with the extraordinary bodily sensations and sexual feelings, which he still attributed to the wicked dentist. He wrote long querulous letters to a friend outside prison about the cruelty of the prison authorities in locking him up with 'sex maniacs'. Such was his condition when interviewed three years and eleven months after conviction.

Case 68

At the age of fifty-one, on the occasion of his twenty-fifth conviction for petty thieving, this man was sentenced to seven years' preventive detention. He had previously been given sentences of imprisonment totalling over thirty years.

On passing through the allocation centre, he was not thought psychotic, although the psychologist noted 'generalised paranoid ideas' and 'a tendency to dissociation of ideas and confabulations'. Two years later, a note in the prison file recorded that he was 'vague and ponderous in his style of writing, using words that are mis-spelt and entirely out of place, and anything but rational in his thinking. No trouble here, but gets vague and queer ideas about his correspondence.'

At interview, he looked untidy and appeared thoroughly confused and unable to give a coherent account of himself. His letters, which were written in a shaky, almost indecipherable scrawl, made no sense. One of them seemed to be appealing for friends of his childhood to be traced.

His answers were at times completely off the point and at other times apposite. For example, asked to repeat a four-digit number backwards he responded with a string of letters and the comment 'I'm trying to run them out on single numbers'. Asked to try again, he repeated a six-digit number backwards without error. Asked to explain the correspondence lessons he was reading, he responded with a spate of confused jargon verging on gibberish. Some of his responses to a request to explain the meaning of simple proverbs were suggestive of schizophrenia. For example:

Too many cooks spoil the broth. 'Too many persons would interfere with another person's personal life and ruin it. It could be that way.'

No delusions or hallucinations were elicited, and on the basis of the interview alone it was impossible to decide whether he was suffering from a functional psychosis or from dementia due to some destructive brain disease.

Case 84

A married man aged fifty-two with twenty-two convictions for offences against property, mostly of a petty nature, such as stealing bicycles. On the last occasion he had taken some articles from a house. Before leaving, and for no understandable reason, he had placed a burning coal on top of a chair.

Although of low average intelligence (I.Q. 93), he had such a poor memory and gave such a confused account of himself that he seemed more like a borderline mental defective.

He had been separated from his wife for many years, but he professed continued interest in her and the children, and spoke of hoping for a reunion. His wife, who seemed a straightforward informant, asserted that he had been persistently unfaithful with prostitutes, had frequently deserted the home, and had never shown any interest in their children. He described various employments he had followed, but from his wife's testimony and the evidence of the police reports it seemed he had never stayed at any job for long, apparently preferring to idle about streets and cafés. He was universally described as cheerful and placid in temperament.

He told the psychiatrist that, apart from childish escapades, he only started thieving as a result of unemployment and lack of money during his early married life, and that he 'carried on' in later years because unhappy relations with his wife prevented him from settling down.

When interviewed, he seemed quite preoccupied with the delusory idea that he had some mortal disease, perhaps a lung cancer, which the prison authorities were hiding from him. He said he had heard the prison officers and the other prisoners whispering among themselves about it.

Only that morning he had heard an officer remark, 'The only thing to do is to let him go and die in peace at home,' and he was sure that the man referred to was himself. On another occasion he had heard a man say, 'I suppose they'll take him off and give him a shot of cocaine, just so as to say they've done something for him.' The psychiatrist sent for his medical notes, looked at them in his presence, and assured him that the radiological report stated clearly that he had no chest disease. Interviewed again after the lunch-break this reassurance proved quite ineffective, for he had heard more whisperings and it was now plain to him that there must be a conspiracy to keep the truth out of his medical records.

The prison hospital notes recorded similar complaints a year previous. He was then diagnosed as having a 'schizoid reaction of short duration'. Seemingly the delusory ideas were now recurring, perhaps with greater intensity.

Appendix II

LIST OF CASES CITED IN THE TEXT

Case	Page	Case	Page
1	35–7	61	64–5
2	14	62	8, 92
3	72–4	63	14, 58, 89
4	43, 58	64	16
5	38–9	65	8, 23–4
6	44–5, 51	66	22, 92
7	8, 28–30, 48	67	59, 86–7, 92
8	49–50	68	54, 89, 111–12
9	41–2	69	5, 89
13	45, 46	70	14
14	8	71	22, 89
16	22	72	24–5, 58, 89
18	78	73	88
19	8, 14	74	88, 91
20	8, 46	75	8, 92, 93–5
22	48	76	89–90
24	48	77	10, 58, 88
25	58	78	78, 88, 91
27	45, 46–7	79	52, 54–5, 88
29	42, 52, 54	81	10, 14, 89, 98
33	5, 48	82	88
34	51, 78	83	13, 53, 109–10
35	47, 58, 78	84	54, 78, 89, 112–13
36	52, 69, 74–5	85	10, 89
38	42, 45, 47	86	97–8
44	14	87	14, 42, 53, 110
45	8	88	13, 64, 91
46	45	89	55
49	8, 37	90	14, 58, 88
50	47	91	53, 111
51	51, 53, 109	92	92
52	58	93	14
54	98	94	15, 59, 69–71, 85
55	30–1	95	53, 78, 89, 101
56	14, 16, 67–8, 78, 88	96	14, 56–7, 88
57	59, 88	97	10, 58, 89
58	13, 14, 59, 68–9, 78, 87–8	98	13
59	89, 99	99	14, 59, 92–3, 96, 98
60	14, 92	100	59, 98

APPENDIX III

TABLE 1.—COMPARISONS OF SAMPLES OF RECIDIVISTS

	50 Intermittent recidivists	50 P. D. s (West)	100 P. D. s (Taylor)	178 P. D. s (Hammond)
Mean number of convictions per man	11.7	13.8	17.5	16.5
Percentage convicted as juveniles	32	46	-	50
Mean number of previous imprisonments*	6.9	8.8	11	10.2
Mean length in years of present sentence	2.0	7.8	8.0	8.6
Mean age on first conviction	19.7	18.3	18.5	17
Mean age at latest conviction	43	40	40	42
Mean time at liberty preceding present conviction (in months)	17.5	10.9	9	9
Percentage at liberty not more than two years preceding present conviction	76	86	96	90
Mean value of property involved in main charges in present conviction (when known or when applicable)	£481	£130	£280	£160
Percentage unskilled workers	42	64	65	63
Percentage unmarried or apart from wife	68	90	86	77
Percentage who have had a period on probation	42	36	not given	35
Percentage from incomplete or broken homes	46	54	40	approx. 40

* Excluding Borstal, corrective training and preventive detention.

TABLE 2.—PRISONERS BY AGE AT TIME OF FIRST CONVICTION

Age in years	10 to 13	14 to 16	17 to 19	20 to 22	23 to 25	26 to 30	over 30	Total cases
Intermittent recidivists	7	9	16	5	5	5	3	50
Preventive detainees	13	10	10	5	7	2	3	50

TABLE 3.—PREVIOUS SENTENCES

	Percentage of cases who had experienced					
	Approved school and Borstal	Approved school only	Borstal only	Corrective training	Preventive detention	Probation
50 Intermittent recidivists	6%	4%	14%	6%	0%	42%
West 50 P.D.s.	20%	4%	18%	22%	18%	36%
Taylor 100 P.D.s.	25%	5%	16%	20%	19%	not given

TABLE 4.—ANALYSIS OF CONVICTIONS

	Number of occasions convicted	
	50 Intermittent recidivists	50 Preventive detainees
On charges of offences against property	486 (83%)	631 (91.2%)
On charges of sexual offences	16 (2.7%)	22 (3.2%)
On charge of physical violence to others (excluding sex)	16 (2.7%)	17 (2.5%)
On various other charges	82 (14%)	50 (7.2%)
Total number of occasions convicted	585	692

N.B. The percentages do not total 100 on account of a minority of convictions including charges of more than one type, and a few charges of violence (e.g. robbery) being classed also among the offences against property.

TABLE 5.—ANALYSIS OF MAIN CHARGES AT LATEST CONVICTION

Categories of offences on main charges	50 Intermittent recidivists	50 Preventive detainees	Taylor 100 P.D.s	Hammond 178 P.D.s
Breaking and entering, or ditto with larceny	12	26	40	48.4%
Larceny or attempted larceny only	20	9	37	23.0%
Receiving, fraud or false pretences	10	11	16	21.3%
Sexual offences	3	2	3	2.2%
Violence to persons	3	0	8	4.5%
Other offences	3	2	0	0.6%
Total	51*	50	104	100.%

* N.B. One man was charged with both larceny and indecent assault.

TABLE 6.—VALUE OF PROPERTY INVOLVED IN MAIN CHARGES AT LATEST CONVICTIONS (where known and when applicable)

	Number of offenders		
Value of property	50 Intermittent recidivists	West 50 P.D.s	Taylor 100 P.D.s
£1 or less	2 (5.0%)	6 (13%)	13 (16%)
Over £1, up to £10	8 (20%)	10 (22%)	23 (28%)
Over £10, up to £100	11 (27%)	19 (41%)	25 (31%)
Over £100, up to £500	10 (24%)	7 (15%)	14 (17%)
Over £500, up to £1000	7 (17%)	3 (6.5%)	0 (0%)
Over £1000	3 (7.3%)	1 (2.2%)	6 (7.4%)
Total cases	41 (100%)	46 (100%)	81 (100%)

Table 7.—Value of Property Concerned in Offences 'Taken into Consideration' at Latest Conviction

Value	50 Intermittent recidivists		West. 50 preventive detainees	
	Number of men	Total number of offences taken into consideration	Number of men	Total number of offences taken into consideration
0	46	0	29	0
Up to £10	0	0	2	10
Over £10 to £100	1	21	6	68
Over £100 to £500	1	3	7	191
Over £500 to £1,000	2	50	4	304
Over £1,000	0	0	2	356
Total prisoners	50	74	50	929

Table 8.—Classification of Occupations of Prisoners and their Fathers (or Guardians)

	50 Intermittent recidivists		West. 50 preventive detainees	
	Occupation Fathers	Occupation Prisoners	Occupation Fathers	Occupation Prisoners
Skilled	23%	6%	20%	12%
Semi-skilled	47%	40%	56%	26%
Unskilled	30%	54%	24%	62%
Total cases	47	50	45	50

Table 9.—Distribution of Intelligence Quotients of Preventive Detainees

	Dull (I.Q. 80 or less)	Dull normal (I.Q.81 to 90)	Average (I.Q.91 to 109)	Above average (I.Q.110 or above)	Total cases
Number of cases	4	8	26	12	50

Table 10.—Prisoners Classified by Size of Family and Position in Birth Order of Siblings (including only those reared at least in part by their own parents and counting full siblings who survived beyond infancy)

Number of siblings in family	1 (i.e.only children)	2	3	4	5	6	7	8	9	10	11	12	Total
Number of prisoners from families of these sizes	6	20	16	5	9	12	3	8	5	2	0	2	88
Number who occupied eldest or youngest positions	-	-	10	1	3	5	0	1	2	1	0	0	23

TABLE 10A

Family size	Prisoners	Lees' sample of juvenile delinquents
1, i.e. only children	6 (6.8%)	10 (4.9%)
2	20 (22.7%)	34 (16.5%)
3 to 6	42 (47.7%)	130 (63.1%)
more than 6	20 (22.7%)	32 (15.6%)
Total	88 (100%)	206 (100%)

TABLE 11.—MARITAL STATUS OF HABITUAL PRISONERS

Percentage	Single	Divorced or separated	Married and living with wife	Widower	Cohabiting	Known to be fathers
West. 50 P.D.s	50	44	8	2	8	40
Taylor 100 P.D.s	41	45	15	1	2	34
50 Intermittent recidivists	26	42	32	6	14	54

N.B. The figures for marital status do not total 100 per cent on account of multiple marriages, producing individuals who have been both widowers and divorcees. There is a slight over-lap between the 'single' and the 'cohabiting' categories.

TABLE 12.—PERSONALITY DEVIATION AND SOCIAL DATA

(The figures in each cell represent total numbers of prisoners. The figures following in brackets represent the numbers for the intermittent recidivist and preventive detainee groups respectively.)

Number of prisoners who were:	Non-deviants (I.R. + P.D)	Active-agressive deviants (I.R. + P.D)	Passive-inadequate deviants (I.R. + P.D)	Total cases (I.R. + P.D)
Convicted on more than ten occasions	5 (3+2)	22 (8+14)	34 (11+23)	61 (22+39)
Unmarried	1 (1+0)	8 (1+7)	29 (11+18)	38 (13+25)
Solitary individuals	0 (0+0)	6 (3+3)	32 (12+20)	38 (15+23)
Living with wife	9 (6+3)	6 (6+0)	5 (4+1)	20 (16+4)
Satisfactory employees	4 (2+2)	3 (2+1)	5 (3+2)	12 (7+5)
Satisfactory servicemen	4 (4+0)	1 (1+0)	6 (5+1)	11 (10+1)
Excessive drinkers	2 (2+0)	13 (6+7)	19 (12+7)	34 (20+14)
With psychiatric symptoms	.2 (1+1)	13 (6+7)	37 (14+23)	52 (21+31)
Separated from parents under 15	4 (2+2)	18 (10+8)	29 (11+18)	51 (23+28)
Total	12 (8+4)	36 (19+17)	52 (23+29)	100 (50+50)

Table 13.—Personality Deviations and Scale of Offences

Personality type:	Value of property involved in main charges at latest conviction (or at latest to which a property value is applicable)					
	Not more than £50			Over £50		
	Intermittent recidivists	Preventive detainees	All prisoners	Intermittent recidivists	Preventive detainees	All prisoners
Non-deviant	2	1	3	6	3	9
Active-aggressive	9	8	17	10	9	19
Passive-inadequate	13	21	34	9	7	16
Total cases	24	30	54*	25	19	44*

* The two cases not included in this tabulation had convictions only for sexual offences.

Table 14.—Personality Type in Relation to Large-scale Offences and False Pretences

Personality classification	Total cases	Number of cases with main charge at latest conviction concerning property valued over £300	Habitual false-pretenders
Non-deviant	12 (8 + 4)	8 (5 + 3)	2 (1 + 1)
Active-aggressive	36 (19 + 17)	9 (6 + 3)	9 (1 + 8)
Inadequate	52 (23 + 29)	0	4 (1 + 3)
Total	100	17	15

TABLE 15.—FIFTY RECIDIVISTS AT WANDSWORTH

Intervals at liberty between convictions

(Figures are given in months. Those fulfilling the criteria of a 'gap' in heavy type. Gaps considered genuinely crime-free marked with an asterisk)

Case Number	
1	1. 2. 3. 6. 0. 3. 20. 0. 4. 1. 9. 9. **157.*** 15. 0. 5. 2. 2. 1. 2. 0. 2. 1. 1. 0. 0. 0. 22. 1. 2. 0. 3. 14. 0. 0.
2	21. 4. **100.*** 25. 42. 9. 10. 27.
3	34. **73.** 17. 4. 4. 7. 1.
4	2. **96.*** 1. 2. 5. 1. 3. 5. 1. 2. 0. 9. 2. 6. 10. 0.
5	2. 9. 4. 20. 10. 18. **73.** 4. 8.
6	35. 2. 5. 7. 3. 5. 10. 10. 12. 10. 7. 22. 11. **58.*** 51.
7	13. 0. 0. **106.*** **103.*** 32. 5.
8	27. 6. **58.*** 7.
9	11. 38. 9. **58.** 20. 31. 24. 35.
10	31. 17. **90.** **133.** 42. **56.** 7.
11	1. 9. 48. 23. 37. 1. **75.*** 11.
12	26. 1. 27. 31. 6. **146.*** 0. 9. 5. 24.
13	119. **54.*** 1. **112.*** 3.
14	9. 21. 5. **143.** 8. 16. **83.** 46. 14. 13. 16.
15	1. 1. 11. **87.** 15. 40. 33. 18.
16	94. 9. 11. 4. 4. 0. 5. **79.*** 23. 15. 59.
17	130. 11. 4. 2. **78.*** 3.
18	20. 6. 1. 13. 5. **66.** 37.
19	13. **78.*** 26. 5. 18. 83.
20	28. **54.** **121.*** 18. 44. 10. 6. 14. 43.
21	36. 7. 2. 29. 10. 14. 13. 23. 29. 10. 27. 12. **98.** 30. 0. 0. 5.
22	0. 34. 9. 4. 8. **79.*** 15. 14.
23	11. 2. 30. **191.** 23.
24	12. 0. 4. **114.*** 8. 4.
25	52. 13. **66.*** 5. 0. 0. 6.
26	7. 3. **67.** 16.
27	54. **74.*** 6.
28	26. 9. **105.** 2. 25.
29	15. **54.*** 3. 32. 0. 4. 2. 2. 2. 1. 1. **94.*** 2. 1. 3. 0. 3. 0. 1. 1. 1. 2. 2.
30	4. 6. 1. 21. **61.*** 13. 23.
31	6. 4. 5. **121.*** 19. 2. 0. 8. 15. 47. 1.
32	1. 13. **70.*** 14. **68.*** 0.
33	81. 8. **96.*** 28. 7.
34	1. **59.** 20. **118.*** 1. 1.
35	5. 4. 9. 16. 2. 0. 11. **66.** 10. 17. 11. 12. 7. **100.*** 7. 0. 3.
36	16. 5. 31. 28. **95.** 6. 2.
37	0. **71.** 21. 12. **63.** **56.** 21. 11. **70.** 5. 8. 17. 5.
38	15. **92.*** 42. 9. 10. **71.*** 7. 5. 23.
39	4. 2. 5. 2. 2. 2. 2. 1. 15. 7. 24. 5. 0. 33. 9. **110.*** **67.*** 80.
40	105. 2. 0. 7. 0. 12. 5. 1. 0. 26. 15. 25. 5. 2. 1. 1. 1. 0. 1. 5. **103.** 1. 4. 1. 1. 5. 2.
41	17. 33. 14. 7. 8. 36. 18. **61.** 10. 23. 38. 0.
42	8. 2. 3. 0. 1. 3. 4. 3. 8. **76.*** 15. 5. 30. 4. 18. 5.
43	26. 21. **71.*** 3. 9.
44	30. **89.** 6.
45	20. **93.** 46.
46	16. 14. 8. 2. **51.*** 5. 6. 4. 1. 15. 26. 34. 1.
47	47. 5. 0. 0. 10. 0. 0. **59.** 1. 5. 6.
48	6. 43. 32. 11. 19. 0. 7. **66.** 17. 25. 65.
49	3. 2. 8. 9. 21. 32. **51.** 12. 7. 41.
50	1. 8. 3. 0. 16. **75.*** 3. 8.

N.B. Convictions as juveniles were not counted in this tabulation, and convictions for breach of probation were also discounted because they referred to previous offences for which convictions were already on record.

TABLE 16.—FIFTY INTERMITTENT RECIDIVISTS

	Durations of intervals at liberty between convictions											
Duration of interval in months	0-12	13-24	25-36	37-48	49-60	61-72	73-84	85-96	97-108	109-120	121 or more	Total
Number of such intervals in the adult records of 50 prisoners	287	71	40	17	16	16	14	11	8	5	8	493

TABLE 17.—GENUINE AND PSEUDO GAPS IN THE CRIMINAL HISTORIES OF FIFTY RECIDIVISTS

Personality classification	Prisoners with one or more genuine gaps	Prisoners with no genuine gap	Total
Non-deviant	3	5	8
Active-aggressive	9	10	19
Passive-inadequate	18	5	23
All cases	30	20	50

TABLE 18.—PERSONALITY RATINGS OF FIFTY PREVENTIVE DETAINEES

Case Number	51	52	53	54	55	56	57	58	59	60	61	62	63	64
Personality classification	I	A	A	I	I	A	I	A	I	A	A	A	I	I
Passive inadequacy	2	0	0	2	2	0	2	0	1	0	0	0	2	2
Neurotic tendency or psychosis (P)	P	0	0	2	1	0	2	0	1	0	0	0	2	0
Impulsive aggression	0	1	0	1	0	0	1	0	0	0	2	0	0	0
Emotional indifference	0	1	5	0	0	5	1	6	4	0	0	2	1	3

Case Number	65	66	67	68	69	70	71	72	73	74	75	76	77	78	79	80	81	82	83	84	85
Personality classification	N	I	I	I	A	I	I	I	I	I	N	I	A	I	I	I	N	N	I	I	A
Passive inadequacy	0	1	1	2	0	2	2	2	2	2	0	2	0	2	2	2	0	0	1	1	0
Neurotic tendency or psychosis (P)	0	2	2	P	0	1	2	0	0	0	1	1	2	1	1	0	0	0	P	P	1
Impulsive aggression	0	0	0	0	0	0	1	0	0	0	0	0	0	0	0	0	0	1	0	0	0
Emotional indifference	1	3	0	3	0	0	0	0	6	4	0	2	6	0	0	0	4	0	5	2	4

Case Number	86	87	88	89	90	91	92	93	94	95	96	97	98	99	100
Personality classification	A	I	A	I	A	I	I	I	A	A	I	A	A	I	I
Passive inadequacy	1	2	0	2	0	2	2	1	0	0	2	0	0	2	1
Neurotic tendency or psychosis (P)	1	P	1	1	1	P	2	1	0	P	2	1	0	0	1
Impulsive aggression	0	0	2	0	0	0	0	1	1	0	0	0	1	0	0
Emotional indifference	4	2	3	0	5	0	0	4	6	5	0	6	2	1	2

N=Non-deviant I=Inadequate A=Active-aggressive

TABLE 19.—RELATION BETWEEN PSYCHIATRIC SYMPTOMS AND EMOTIONAL INDIFFERENCE

		Emotional indifference score			Number of cases
		0 or 1	2 or 3	4,5 or 6	
Neurotic score	0	9	3	7	19
	1	6	3	6	15
	2	7	1	1	9
Psychotics		2	3	2	7
Number of cases		24	10	16	50

TABLE 20.—RELATION BETWEEN PASSIVE-INADEQUACY AND EMOTIONAL INDIFERRENCE

		Emotional indifference score			Number of cases
		0 or 1	2 or 3	4,5 or 6	
Passive inadequacy score	0	7	3	10	20
	1	1	3	4	8
	2	16	4	2	22
Number of cases		24	10	16	50

TABLE 21.—LIE-SCORE RESULTS

Psychiatrist's rating on persistent lying		Cases with lie-score	
		Less than 18	Over 18 (i.e. cases in upper quartile)
Non-liars	0 (a)	18 (a: 26)	3 (a: 3)
Moderate liars	1 (a, b)	8 (b: 20)	0 (b: 9)
Extreme liars	2 (b)	12	9
Total cases		38	12

Combination (a): $\chi^2 = 5.39$. $P < 0.05$
Combination (b): $\chi^2 = 1.07$. not significant

TABLE 22.—PASSIVE-INADEQUACY AND NEUROTICISM

Psychatrist's rating on passive-inadequacy		All cases cases with N. score * less than 35	over 35	Ten 'liars' excluded cases with N. score less than 40	over 40
Nil	0	10	10	11	5
Moderate	1	7	1	6	0
Extreme	2	8	14	4	14
Total cases		25	25	21	19

$\chi^2 = 12.08$ with 2 deg. freedom
$P < 0.01$

* The neuroticism and the extraversion scores represent a slight modification of the customary scales. Six items of particular significance were presented twice and scored on both occasions, thus increasing the maximum possible score for any one individual from 48 to 60.

TABLE 23.—EXTRAVERSION SCORES RELATED TO EMOTIONAL INDIFFERENCE

Psychiatric rating on emotional indifference		Extraversion score less than 33*	Extraversion score more than 33
No tendency or only slight	(0 or 1)	4	12
Moderate	(2 or 3)	5	5
Severe	(4, 5 or 6)	16	8
Total cases		25	25

$r = 0.30$ $P = 0.05$

TABLE 24.—'F' SCORES RELATED TO INADEQUACY

	F score less than 9	F score greater than 9
Inadequate personality deviants	10	19
Other types	15	6
Total cases	25	25

$\chi^2 = 6.66$ with 1 degree freedom

$P < 0.01$ $r_{tet} = 0.55$

Table 25.—Psychaesthenia Score Related to Inadequacy

	Psychaesthenia (Pt) scores		Psychaesthenia (Pt) scores, eliminating high F scores	
	Under 17	17 or over	Under 17	17 or over
Inadequates	10	19	10	6
Others	15	6	15	4
Total cases	25	25	25	10

Table 26.—Scores on Hysteria Scale and Psychiatric Ratings

Psychiatric ratings		Hy score less than 20		Hy score 20 or over	
Emotional indifference score	0	8	12 (0–1)	11	12 (0–1)
	1	4		1	
	2	4	4 (2–3)	2	6 (2–3)
	3	0		4	
	4	4	8 (4–6)	2	8 (4–6)
	5	3		2	
	6	1		4	
Inadequates		9		20	
Others		15		6	
Neurotic symptoms	0	13		6	
	1	6	11 (1, 2, Psychotics)	9	20 (1, 2, Psychotics)
	2	3		6	
Psychotics		2		5	

Table 27.—Psychopathic Deviate (Pd) Scores and Psychiatric Ratings

Psychiatric ratings		Pd. score less than 22	Pd. score 22 or over
Emotional indifference score	2 or over	13	13
	less than 2	11	13
Lying	0	10	11
	1	4	4
	2	10	11
Inadequates		11	18
Others		13	7

TABLE 28.—FAMILY BACKGROUND, PERSONALITY AND ONSET OF CRIME

(Figures for intermittent recidivists and preventive detainees given side by side. The former enclosed in brackets.)

Family background	Total cases		Number of inadequates		Average score on emotional indifference	Number with a conviction as juveniles		Average age in years at first conviction	
	I.R.	P.D.	I.R.	P.D.	P.D.	I.R.	P.D.	I.R.	P.D.
Class I	(12)	14	(7)	6	2.0	(2)	3	(24.5)	20.4
Class II	(5)	11	(1)	6	3.0	(1)	6	(20.0)	17.9
Class III	(14)	13	(5)	8	2.5	(4)	7	(17.9)	17.8
Class IV	(12)	12	(7)	9	1.2	(6)	7	(18.1)	16.5
All cases	(43)	50	(20)	29	2.2	(13)	23	(20.0)	18.3

PRINTED IN GREAT BRITAIN
BY ROBERT MACLEHOSE AND CO. LTD
THE UNIVERSITY PRESS, GLASGOW